Pacific NORTH WEST Flavors

Pacific NORTH WEST Flavors

150 Recipes from the Region's
Farmland, Coastline, Mountains & Cities

Photographs by Michael Skott
Text by Lori McKean

Clarkson Potter / Publishers
New York

To my father,
who bought me my first camera.
–M. S.

To my mother,
Janet Armstrong Davis,
and her mother, Inez DuPuis,
for teaching me the secrets of their
kitchens. And to the magnificent
guiding spirit of the
Pacific Northwest.
–L.M.

Published by Clarkson N. Potter/Publishers, 201 East 50th Street, New York, New York 10022. Member of the Crown Publishing Group.

Random House, Inc. New York, Toronto, London, Sydney, Auckland

Clarkson N. Potter, Potter, and colophon are trademarks of Clarkson N. Potter, Inc.

Manufactured in China

Book design by Don Morris Design

Library of Congress Cataloging-in-Publication Data

McKean, Lori.

Pacific northwest flavors / text by Lori McKean: photographs by Michael Skott.

p.   cm.

Includes index.

1. Cookery, American—Pacific Northwest style. 2. Northwest, Pacific—Social life and customs. 3. Northwest, Pacific—Description and travel. I. Title.

TX715.2.P32M38   1995

641.59795—dc20   94-4809

                    CIP

ISBN 0-517-57564-7

10 9 8 7 6 5 4 3 2 1

First Edition

Acknowledgments

We would like to thank the many people who contributed to this project: Jerilyn Brusseau; Sinclair and Fredrica Philip; Bonnie and Dennis White; Sally and Roger Jackson and family; Ida Mary, Lloyd Ley, and family; Chris and Alida Latham; Ron and Carrie Zimmerman; Polly Schoonmaker; Mallory Sampson and friends; Peter and Karen Lynn; Jim McCrae; Liz Henderson and John Keen; Andrew Yeoman and Noel Richardson; Veronica Williams; Loragene and Phillip Gaulin; Dan Driscoll; Michael and Rita Pratt; Steve McCarthy and Lucinda Parker; Mary and Fred McCullough and guests, Michael Boyd, Bill, Susan, and Ian Fletcher, The Kroft Family, David Kampiche and Laurie Anderson, Lee Gray, Randy and Kathy Sackett, Sandra and Ken Fein, Elizabeth Fujas and family, and last, but not least, Maria Lara and Bob.

Also, many thanks to all the patient people at Clarkson Potter who believed in this project over the years, especially our editor, Pam Krauss. And to Don Morris, thanks for putting all of the pieces together.

Finally, thanks to Mary Emmerling, Trish Foley, and Martha Stewart.

Introduction

DURING THE COOL DAMP WINTERS of the Pacific Northwest, subtle-flavored root vegetables, wild mushrooms, and truffles lie waiting in the earth, ready to be harvested and cooked into warm, nourishing dishes. Fruit, grape, and nut orchards are pruned in anticipation of large harvests, and farmlands are plowed under, ready to be replanted in the spring with grains and vegetables. Deep in the forests a thick layer of leaves, cedar twigs, and fir needles decomposes softly into the moist earth, providing nutrients for mushrooms, ferns, and wild berries. The frothy Pacific Ocean pounds the coastline, flowing through ribbons of kelp and stirring up food for barnacles, mussels, clams, plus a variety of other fish and shellfish.

As spring approaches, trees and shrubs erupt with vibrant green tufts of leaves and needles. Cocoa-colored morels, golden chanterelles, and tender fiddlehead ferns nudge into the filtered light of the forest beneath a blanket of decayed leaves. Newly tilled fields explode with crops, and rivers rise swiftly with rainwater and snowmelt, awakening salmon fry from their gravel nests under the river floor. Soon these tiny fish will fight their way downriver, past dams and other obstacles, to the ocean, where they will feed and grow into adults.

Eventually the salmon, sometimes weighing as much as ninety pounds, will succumb to their instinctual homing devices and begin battling their way upstream to their birthplace, where they will produce spawn, creating new life before they die.

Many of the flavors associated with Pacific Northwest cuisine evoke the beauty of the untamed land, rivers, lakes, sounds, and ocean. Buttery rich salmon is fruity and musty, redolent of the deep sea, while delicate seafoods like Dungeness crab, scallops, halibut, and perch sparkle with sweet, clean, oceanic flavors. Juicy berries burst in the mouth, releasing flavors of hot summer sun and evergreen-scented air. Wild mushrooms taste earthy and sweet like the decaying loam of the forest floor. Oysters smack of briny saltwater bays and crisp minerals, and wild game resounds with the hearty, robust flavors of the dense forests and rugged mountains.

This is a cuisine that has developed gradually over time—with cooks today creating dishes using many of the same indigenous foods that Native Americans cooked long ago. The region is blessed with an abundance of extraordinary seafoods and a profusion of native fruits and produce, nuts, and wild game. These foods were, and still are, highly revered by the Native Americans, who have lived in the region for thousands of years.

The arrival of non–Native Americans to the Northwest in the mid-1800s brought successive waves of immigrants from Italy, Greece, Scandinavia, Asia, Russia, Spain, Britain, the East Indies, and more. These newcomers welcomed northwestern seafood into their kitchens, incorporating it into the traditional recipes of their homelands. Fresh salmon or sturgeon, for example, might be cooked Mediterranean style in a spicy tomato sauce. Dungeness crab was adorned with homemade mayonnaise and served with buttered brown bread. Fresh

scallops and local fish were often enriched with French-based sauces like hollandaise and béarnaise. Slowly, layer upon layer, like the thick flesh of a Copper River King salmon or the rings of an old-growth cedar, Pacific Northwest cuisine evolved. It continues to evolve, retaining always at its center the integrity of fresh northwestern ingredients.

This book is a collaboration between two Northwesterners. One, Michael, is a recent newcomer, and to his photographer's eye, the region offers an exciting new canvas. As a native of the Northwest, I have spent considerable time on the Oregon Coast, where I live and work. My food memories go back to my childhood in Seattle, where my mother and grandmother, both exceptional cooks, taught me the basics of cookery early on and instilled in me a passion for gathering and cooking a variety of wild Northwest foods.

I remember mushroom "witching" for morels in the virgin cedar forests of Whidbey Island; collecting mussels by moonlight during a stormy winter night on the Oregon Coast; picking and hand-pressing apple cider on a crisp autumn day; hunting for prickly burred chestnuts beneath the trees on a frosty winter morning; digging razor clams barehanded on the Washington

coast; turning buckets of tiny, wild blackberries into pies and jam; and landing my
first salmon in Puget Sound and barbecue-
ing it that evening for dinner.

When Jeanne and Michael relocated to
the Pacific Northwest, from New York
City, they were moved by the rugged mountains, the tremendous forests, and the
island-dotted waters of Puget Sound, all of
which they eagerly explored. On their first
trip to the Northwest, they camped in a
rock outcropping in Washington, where
they dined on smoked salmon and local
beer. That evening, while the rolling Pacific
Ocean lulled them to sleep and the clean,
fresh scent of evergreens filled their lungs,
they realized that, in their hearts, they had
become Northwesterners.

T he Skotts quickly adapted to the
Northwest lifestyle. They learned
to identify and collect wild
greens, mushrooms, and berries. Soon,
Jeanne was canning her own blackberries
and preserving homegrown and local
fruits—putting up jars of butters, jams, and
jellies. Just off their beach, on Orcas Island,
the Skotts now fish for Dungeness crabs
and salmon, with the help of their energetic
son, Alexander. Behind their photography
studio, Michael built a chicken coop, where
they raise a variety of chickens, turkeys, and
Cornish game hens.

While on Orcas, the Skotts dine simply—
usually on farm-raised fruits and vegetables,
home-grown poultry, pasta . . . "I like food
that is simple and easy to prepare," says
Jeanne. "We love dishes like garden salads,
baked chicken, and homemade pizza."

The Skotts also love to barbecue. Their
favorite is fresh salmon, or Ling cod, marinated in tamari sauce and garlic, cooked
slowly over the grill. Just before he places
the fish over the grill, Michael tops the
coals with green alder branches, which have
been soaked in water. This adds a rich
smoky flavor to the fish.

I met Michael and his wife, Jeanne,
shortly after they moved to the
Pacific Northwest. We found that
we shared a keen appreciation for the great
Northwest, especially when it came to food
and cooking. As we traveled throughout the
magnificent region together, the unique culinary history of the area slowly unraveled
through the people we talked to and the
places we visited.

It is impossible to live in the Northwest
and remain unaware of the profound con-
nection between its cuisine and the varied
terrain that inspires it.

The exceptional quality and flavor of
Northwest ingredients demand simplicity.
Anyone who has eaten freshly cooked and
cracked Dungeness crab, nectar-sweet

steamed clams, briny oysters on the half shell, or grilled spring Chinook salmon has experienced Northwest cuisine at its best.

Nothing better expresses the cuisine of this region than the Native American's stick-cooked salmon. The fish is laced between a sturdy split pole with cedar sticks, then the pole is stuck in the ground near a slow-burning fire where the salmon cooks slowly, basting itself with its own oil while absorbing the fragrant smoke of the fire.

The basic premise of good cooking is always to start with the freshest, highest-quality ingredients you can find. The goal in cooking is to showcase the food in the very best way possible to highlight its unique qualities, texture, and flavor. Keep in mind when following these recipes that all cooking is based on improvisation. Recipes are intended to guide and inspire you; ingredient lists are not written in stone. If you feel that a certain fish, vegetable, or herb is better suited to a dish or fresher than the one called for, don't hesitate to substitute.

A painting on the cover of James Beard's autobiography, published in 1964, depicts Beard seated at a table on the seashore facing Tillamook Head, near Seaside, Oregon. One of America's most loved and respected culinary authorities, Beard spent much of his

life on the Oregon coast, of which he wrote, "Those busy days on the Oregon coast left their mark on me, and no place on earth, with the exception of Paris, has done as much to influence my professional life."

The cooking of all who live in the Northwest is inevitably flavored by their experiences here. The recipes included in this book are a combination of our recipes and those of prominent Northwest chefs, farmers, fishermen, oyster growers, innkeepers, cheese makers, and others in the business of growing or producing food. Our love and respect for the land and its products, and of the enthusiastic people who live and work in the Pacific Northwest, provided the inspiration for this book. We hope you will be as inspired as we were by their dedication to producing food of the very highest quality, and by the region that gave them the means to do so.

COASTAL
waters

T SEEMS ONLY FITTING to begin our book with a section on the waters of the Pacific Northwest, where Michael and I live and work. Covering one-third of the planet's surface, the mighty Pacific Ocean breaks on the shores of five separate continents and numerous islands, swelling and receding four times daily according to the rhythms of the sun and moon. Host to more than two hundred species of edible fish and shellfish, including halibut, perch, salmon, smelt, tuna, sea bass, barnacles, mussels, clams, crab, sea urchins, and much more, the ocean is the pulse of the Northwest.

Depending on the season and on the prevailing winds, the Pacific can be as placid as an alpine lake or as violent as a hurricane, with winter storms ravaging the coast at eighty to one hundred miles per hour. Nestled in a thicket of salal and sea grass, protected from the howling wind, one can perch on the crown of a small coastal headland overlooking Silver Point, one of the giant basalt seastacks that stand sentinel over the shores of Cannon Beach, the small coastal town in Oregon, where I have lived for several years.

Native Americans gathered on this headland for an extended period of time to cook and eat. These bits of shell and bone are now the only reminders of the people who once inhabited these shores. The people may be gone but the water remains: Descendants of the few surviving Native Americans of the Pacific Northwest still honor the water in songs and celebrations.

Out of necessity, much of the cookery of the indigenous people revolved around food preservation. Most foods were seasonal and had to be preserved to last through the winter. Before refrigeration this was accomplished in several ways. Fish, berries, and roots were often dried, either whole or mashed, in the sun, by the wind, or by suspending them over a smoky fire. Preserving foods in oil was another common method of preservation. Eulachon oil (pronounced you-li-con), obtained from a very oily species of smelt also known as candlefish, was used as a sort of all-purpose grease for preserving foods or for dipping foods into, much as olive oil is used in the Mediterranean. Whale oil, bear oil, and dogfish oil were also utilized.

With the demise of the native population followed by an onrush of technology, which began during the late 1800s and continued into the mid-1900s, Northwest cuisine went through a dramatic transformation. Influenced in part by the luxuries of transportation, refrigeration, and electricity and by an influx of European and Asian immigrants, the coastal cuisine of the Northwest was no longer defined solely by indigenous foods that were eaten fresh, cooked, or preserved for later use. With the arrival of immigrants from Greece, Italy, Scandinavia, China, and Japan, and many others who came west to mine for gold or to work in the logging, fishing, or transportation industries, came new cooking techniques, spices, and ideas for utilizing the Northwest's seafoods.

The northwestern fishing industry, which has always centered around salmon, has a long and elaborate history beginning with the native people of the region, who fished with gill and seine nets made of wild hemp, tree roots, cedar fibers, or strips of animal hides. Cedar canoes served as their trolling vessels. In the early 1800s, the annual Columbia River salmon catch by the natives was estimated at about 18 million pounds. By the 1820s, the Hudson's Bay Company was established in Astoria, Oregon, and native fishermen began trading salmon for ammunition, corn, tobacco, and other trade goods. Salted and pickled salmon, the staple food products of the Hudson's Bay Company, were exported to places as far away as Hawaii, Australia, England, China, and the East Coast of the United States.

The first cannery along the Columbia River was built in 1866 by brothers William, George, and Robert Hume, third-generation fishermen originally from Maine. By 1881, thirty-five canneries were strung along both sides of the lower Columbia, half of which were founded by the Humes. At first the canneries processed only Chinook salmon, but, due to the Chinook's declining numbers in the 1890s, canneries began experimenting with Coho (silver) salmon and pink (humpbacked) salmon. By 1915, forty-one canneries had been established in the Puget Sound area as well.

Along the Columbia River, many of the salmon canneries were surrounded by villages of Chinese immigrants, who found a livelihood making tin cans for the fisheries. Scraps of tin still sparkle along the shoreline of the Columbia where fishing communities once stood. The 1905 invention of the "Iron Chink," a machine that butchered, cleaned, and prepared salmon for canning, revolutionized the fishing industry, forcing thousands out of work. Today, with a growing concern over freshness and quality, most Northwest fish and shellfish are marketed throughout the country fresh or frozen rather than canned .

Michael and I visited towns, cities, and seaports up and down the 500-mile stretch of Northwest coastline. Many of these towns are centered around the mouths of large Northwest rivers, including the Rogue, Umpqua, and Suislaw rivers of

Above: **A** minus tide on the **N**orthwest coast offers up clams, oysters, mussels, cockles, and more.
Opposite: **A**lexander **S**kott proudly displays his oyster catch.

southern Oregon, the Willapa and Chehalis rivers in southern Washington, the Hoh River, which runs through Washington's northern Olympic Peninsula, and the Fraser River in British Columbia, Canada.

The mighty Columbia River irrigates acres of farmland and orchards throughout Utah, Wyoming, Montana, Idaho, Nevada, Oregon, and Washington. In the last 140 miles the Columbia is fed by the Willamette, Sandy, Lewis, Kalama, Cowlitz, and Clatskanie rivers, as well as by hundreds of smaller rivers and streams, many of which are spawning grounds for the Northwest salmon that battle their way upriver to their birthplace to lay their eggs. This elaborate river system is known as the "Mother of the Great Chinook."

We toured Puget Sound and the San Juan Islands, an expansive filigree of islands, bays, straits, and estuaries that stretches

from southern Washington north to British Columbia. This convoluted coastline, which if laid out straight would stretch some 2,000 miles, is a region of unique ecosystems created by freshwater rivers which empty into saltwater bays, estuaries, and deep, swift-running straits. Oysters, crab, sea urchin, abalone, salmon, and other deep-sea fish are often found in these waters.

Whenever they have time off, the Skotts take their sailboat, the *Lively Lady*, out to Sucia Island, or to points farther north in the Gulf Island, where they watch for orcas and porpoises, or watch for seals riding the whirlpools. If they're lucky enough to catch a Dungeness crab when they're out sailing, Jeanne cracks the crab in half, cleans it, and cooks it in seawater for about five minutes. "It's the best way to cook crab," she says. She serves the crab, aboard ship, with garlic aioli and French bread.

18

A Northwest Indian Salmon Celebration

ONE RAINY SPRING DAY *we joined a small group of Native Americans who were huddled together in a makeshift longhouse erected on the banks of the Klikitat River, a swift-running tributary of the Columbia River in south central Washington. Raindrops pattered steadily on the blue plastic tarps that covered the longhouse, hissing and sputtering as they dropped into the hot coals of the outdoor fire pits over which Chinook salmon, venison, and eel cooked. The longhouse faced the river and the rising sun.*

Chief Wilbur J. Slochish of the Klikitat tribe was raised along the banks of this river and he recognizes places along the river by the trees that still stand. This longhouse was erected beside the tall pine where his childhood home once stood. Chief Wilbur, his family, and friends were gathered to offer prayers to the river in remembrance of Chief Wilbur's brother, Howard Wilson, who had drowned in the river the previous winter while fishing. They came also to offer thanks and prayers to the water in celebration of the first salmon of the season.

The tribal drums pulsed through the air, weaving a backbone through the singsong chanting of the drummers. The ancient songs offered thanks and praise to the water—to the river, to the salmon, and to venison, roots, and berries—to sustenance.

According to tradition, First Salmon Celebrations always begin and end with a toast to the water. A small bite of each of the ceremonial foods is taken before the actual feast begins. Chief Wilbur, a wise and gentle man, led the ceremony that day, introducing each of the sacred foods as they were served with the ringing of a small bell followed by words of thanks and praise spoken in his native tongue. A bite of salmon followed the water. Venison was next, followed by the first roots of the season, then wild berries.

When the feast ended, everyone seated in the longhouse was poured another sip of water. Silently we turned toward the river, watching it through a curtain of rain while the drumming and singing resumed in the background.

"The water is our most important resource," said Chief Wilbur. *"That's why water has to come first, then the salmon."*

Sometimes, Michael heads off by himself on a kayaking trip. "I love to travel with great food," he says, recalling one four-day excursion for which he packed in cracked crab, chicken breast, fresh shrimp, wine, and rice, among other goodies. "My secret, without refrigeration, is to keep reheating the food each night," he says. "There's no need to eat packaged foods when you're out in the wilderness."

Nearly everyone who lives in the Pacific Northwest has special memories of the magnificent waters of the region. Often, it is the water that draws people to the Northwest and that provides inspiration for their work

and play. People whose livelihoods revolve around the waters literally glow with pride when they talk about the fish and shellfish harvested from the seas, lakes, and rivers. In the course of our travels we met oyster growers, fishermen, shrimpers, crabbers, and clammers, all of whom exuded passion and enthusiasm.

The recipes in this section, many of which came from people we met, range from homey seafood stews to elegant dishes like Smoked Black Cod in Ginger Broth and Dungeness Crab and Spinach Raviolis. All of the dishes celebrate the delicious bounty of the waters of the Pacific Northwest.

Corn and Oyster Chowder
Serves 4

Hardly anything is more satisfying on a blustery winter day than a bowl of steaming oyster chowder. Jeanne Skott adds sweet corn, bacon, and diced potatoes to this hearty soup, which she sometimes makes with clams instead of oysters.

    1   tablespoon olive oil
    1   medium onion, diced
    5   thick slices bacon
    2   medium new potatoes, diced
   12   medium oysters, scrubbed
    3   tablespoons all-purpose flour
    1   cup half-and-half
        Salt and freshly ground black pepper
        Kernels from two ears of fresh corn
          (about 1½ cups)
    2   tablespoons chopped parsley

Heat the oil in a large saucepan over medium heat and sauté the onion until translucent and slightly golden; set aside. In a separate skillet, sauté the bacon until crisp. Drain the bacon on paper towels and tear into ½-inch pieces. Place the diced potatoes in a saucepan, cover with water, and cook until they can just be pierced with a fork. Drain the potatoes, reserving one cup of the potato water. Place the oysters in a large saucepan with ¼ cup water and steam over high heat until they just open (about 10 minutes). Strain the liquid and reserve.

Add the flour to the sautéed onions and, stirring constantly, cook them over medium heat until foamy. Stir in the reserved oyster liquid and potato water and mix well. Add the oysters and the half-and-half. Stir in the corn and the bacon and cook until heated through (do not allow this to come to a boil). Season to taste with salt and pepper. Garnish each serving with chopped parsley.
Recommended wines: *Chardonnay, Pinot Gris*

Fish Stock
Makes 3 to 4 cups

Lori was very fortunate to attend the Ballymaloe Cookery School near a small fishing village on the southwestern tip of Ireland. The school's recipe for fish stock is simple to prepare and delicious. This recipe takes only 20 minutes to make, and if you can obtain lots of fresh fish bones from your fishmonger it's worth making two or three times the recipe and freezing the extra stock. Then next time you need fish stock you'll be all set. If you can't obtain fish bones or simply don't have time to make it, bottled clam juice can be substituted.

   2¼ pounds fish bones, preferably halibut,
          sole, snapper, cod, or other white fish
    2   tablespoons unsalted butter
    1   cup diced onion
    ½   cup dry white wine
    4   peppercorns
        Bouquet garni consisting of a thyme
          sprig, 4 to 5 parsley sprigs, a small
          piece of celery, and a tiny scrap of
          bay leaf

Chop the bones into pieces small enough to fit in a large saucepan. Wash thoroughly under cold running water until no trace of blood remains. Melt the butter in a saucepan over medium heat. Add the onions and sweat them over a gentle heat until soft but not browned, about 10 minutes. Add the bones to the saucepan. Stir well and cook briefly, about 2 minutes.

Add the wine and boil the mixture until only about 2 tablespoons of liquid remain, about 5 minutes. Add cold water to cover, the peppercorns, and the bouquet garni. Bring the mixture to a boil and skim the foam off the top. Reduce the heat and simmer 20 minutes, skimming often. Strain the stock through a fine sieve and discard the bones.

The Wild Gourmet

LEE GRAY, "THE WILD GOURMET," forages his way through the tide pools, seas, and forests of the Pacific Northwest gathering wild mushrooms, edible seaweeds, wild greens, and shellfish, which he supplies to restaurants and specialty markets.

"Sometimes," Gray says, "I can almost hear the mushrooms calling to me. Oyster mushrooms have a sweet anise scent and I can literally follow my nose right to the spot where they're growing." Whenever he collects wild foods, Gray is careful not to deplete an entire crop, ensuring that the mushrooms or sea life will continue to reproduce.

In addition to oyster mushrooms Gray also collects Boletus edulis, also known as cèpes or porcini, and chanterelles, sweet apricot-scented mushrooms, which, according to Gray, often sprout just after a lightning storm. Gray also harvests wild greens and edible plants, including tender plant shoots like those of blackberry and thimbleberry. "You can steam these just like asparagus and they're quite delicious," he says. From the sea Gray forages edible seaweeds, including giant bullwhip kelp, sea lettuce, red laver, and miniature sea palms (which make unique swizzle sticks). He also collects underutilized varieties of Northwest shellfish, including ocean mussels, barnacles, and sea urchins.

Gray conceived of the idea for his unique business while living in a rock cave above the ocean on the Oregon coast.

"After living and working for twenty years in the film and restaurant industries in Los Angeles I needed a sabbatical," he recalls. Each evening in his cave Gray prepared an elaborate candlelit dinner. Dressed in a velvet dinner jacket and seated at a lace-covered table (a wire spool), he dined on freshly caught seafood, wild greens, and mushrooms while overlooking the Pacific Ocean.

Miniature sea palm (*Postelsia palmaeformis*) is one variety of seaweed Lee Gray collects.
Opposite: **Wild Mushroom and Seafood Chowder.**

Wild Mushroom and Seafood Chowder
Serves 4 to 6

Chef and forager Lee Gray uses wild lobster mushrooms for this creamy chowder, but other mushrooms like chanterelles, *Boletus edulis*, or shiitake, would work, too.

  24 *small mussels, cleaned and debearded*
  ½ *cup shredded smoked salmon*
  2 *garlic cloves, minced*
  2 *tablespoons unsalted butter*
  1 *green pepper, diced*
  1 *stalk celery, chopped*
  1 *cup diced wild mushrooms*
  1 *large onion, diced*
  2 *cups Fish Stock (page 21)*
  ½ *cup mussel juice*
  2 *medium potatoes, diced*
  2 *tablespoons cornstarch*
2½ *cups milk*
    Salt and pepper to taste
    Sorrel or parsley leaves for garnish

In a large saucepan, bring approximately 2 inches of water to a hard boil over high heat. Add the mussels, cover, and cook for 6 to 10 minutes, or until they are just open. Remove the mussels with tongs and set aside to cool. Once they are cool enough to handle, remove the mussels from their shells. Strain the mussel broth through a fine sieve, reserving ½ cup of the liquid. In a large skillet, sauté the smoked salmon and garlic in the butter over medium heat. Add the green pepper, celery, mushrooms, and onion and continue cooking, stirring occasionally, until the vegetables are cooked through (about 10 minutes). Meanwhile, combine the fish stock and the mussel juice in a large stockpot. Bring the stock to a boil over high heat. Add the potatoes, reduce the heat, and simmer the until the potatoes are tender. Add the sautéed vegetables to the stock. Remove the soup from the heat.

Place the cornstarch in a mixing bowl and gradually whisk in ½ cup of the milk to form a smooth mixture. Gradually stir this mixture into the chowder, returning it to the heat and bringing it gently to a boil. Simmer the chowder for about 10 minutes, or until the seafood is heated through. Add salt and pepper to taste. Ladle the chowder into warm serving bowls and garnish each serving with a sorrel or parsley leaf.
Recommended wines: *Pinot Gris, Chenin Blanc, Gamay Beaujolais*

Matsutake Mushrooms in Seaweed Broth
Serves 4

This recipe from the Sooke Harbour House in Sooke, British Columbia, calls for dried *Laminaria saccharina* seaweed, a type of kelp also known as kombu or sugar wrack. Laminaria seaweed is commonly available in Asian markets or specialty stores, as are mirin and white miso. The salty sea flavor of this nutritious broth, which needs to be prepared the night before, highlights the unique peppery flavor of Matsutake (*Armillaria ponderosa*) mushrooms.

  4 *ounces Matsutake mushrooms*
3½ *cups Kelp Stock (recipe follows)*
  1 *tablespoon white miso (shiro)*
  6 *green onions, sliced into 1½-inch pieces*
  2 *tablespoons mirin (sweet sake)*
  2 *tablespoons minced fresh cilantro leaves*
    Whole cilantro leaves, for garnish

Use a soft mushroom brush or pastry brush to clean the mushrooms. Trim off about ¼ inch from the bottom of the stalks. Slice into ¼-inch-thick pieces.

Bring the kelp stock to a full boil over high heat in a medium saucepan. Meanwhile, soften the miso by whisking it with 3 tablespoons of the hot broth in a bowl until smooth; set aside.

Sooke Harbour House

A STURDY FISHING BOAT rolls and heaves with the ebb and flow of ocean swells just off the west coast of Vancouver Island, British Columbia, in the Strait of Juan de Fuca.

From the open stern of the boat, Sinclair Philip, the owner of the Sooke Harbour House Inn, plunges head first into the cold, briny sea.

The whitewashed ocean floor is dimpled and pockmarked like the moon, and nestled into its craters and crevices are hundreds of sea urchins—spiny porcupinesque sunbursts of red, green, and purple—and a surprising number of large, shoe-sized abalone. Using a large knife, Sinclair pries the spiny urchins and stubborn abalone from the rocks, filling a long purse-like basket.

Later, he empties his catch into the large saltwater fish tank located just behind his restaurant's kitchen. He points out the other creatures sharing the space—sea cucumbers, crabs, pink swimming scallops, and geoducks—all of which will soon be cooked and served at the restaurant.

Sinclair's wife, Frederica, who has been busy decorating the dining room with brilliant bouquets of edible flowers, takes a short break to walk us through the edible gardens, pointing out flowers, berries, herbs, and vegetables while Sinclair rattles off their Latin names as well as the history and lore of each plant.

Frederica was raised in the French countryside and Sinclair grew up in the city of Vancouver, B.C., yet both developed an appreciation for simply prepared, high-quality foods early on; Sinclair earned pocket money by fishing for skate and crab, which he sold door to door.

At their restaurant the Philips insist on serving only locally raised food of the highest quality at the peak of its season. Seafoods are all collected from the local waters, often by Sinclair himself. Free-range chickens and their eggs, Muscovy duck, pheasant, rabbit, and lamb are all raised locally on organic farms and greens, herbs, berries, and edible flowers are harvested fresh from the gardens just before serving.

When the stock reaches the boil, reduce the heat to medium. Add the mushrooms, green onions, and mirin. Add the miso, being careful not to cook it more than a few minutes for it will become bitter. Simmer the broth for 2 to 3 minutes, until the vegetables are heated through. Stir in the cilantro. Serve in preheated bowls and garnish with whole cilantro leaves.

Recommended beverage: *Sake*

Kelp Stock
Makes 4 cups

1⅓ ounces dried Laminaria seaweed (kombu)
1 quart cold water

Wipe the seaweed with a damp cloth to clean it. Fill a large bowl with the cold water and add the seaweed. Let stand at room temperature overnight. Remove the seaweed and, if desired, reserve for use in other dishes.

Creamy Sea Urchin Bisque
Serves 4

Sea urchin is considered a delicacy and an aphrodisiac in the Orient, where it fetches high prices. Each sea urchin holds 5 golden petal-shaped roe sacs, which are easily removed by opening the center of the underside of the urchin with a sharp knife and scooping out the roe. The flavorful urchin roe has an initial taste of the sea which slides into egg yolk and wild mushrooms. Chef-owner Sinclair Philip of the Sooke Harbour House often harvests these tiny purple orbs from the water right in front of the inn.

4 *fresh sea urchins, to yield approximately 10 ounces roe*
5 *tablespoons unsalted butter*
6 *shallots, minced*
¾ *cup Gewürztraminer wine or dry pear cider*
1 *cup Fish Stock (page 21)*
1 *cup whipping cream*
4 *2-inch squares freshly harvested sea lettuce*
8 *chives, cut into 1-inch lengths*

Using a sharp knife, cut through the center of the underside portion of each urchin. Scoop out the five orange-yellow roe sacs and discard the remaining portion of the urchin. Reserving 4 of the roe sacs for garnish, puree the remaining roe in a blender or food processor until smooth.

Melt 4 tablespoons of the butter in a medium saucepan over medium heat. Add the shallots and cook for about 5 minutes, or until they become translucent. Add ½ cup of the wine and bring the mixture to a boil for about one minute. Whisk in the fish stock and the whipping cream, mixing well. Simmer the soup over medium heat for about 5 minutes, stirring occasionally. Remove the pan from the heat. Stir in the

Sinclair Philip emerges from the briny sea with a spiny sea urchin, from which he scoops out the tasty roe—caviar on the beach. The roe also goes into his **Creamy Sea Urchin Bisque,** *opposite.*

sea urchin puree and the remaining ¼ cup wine, and set the mixture aside.

Melt the remaining tablespoon of butter in a frying pan over low heat. Warm the sea lettuce and the urchin roe garnish for about 30 seconds, or until warmed through. Ladle the soup into warm serving bowls and spoon the sea lettuce and urchin roe decoratively in the center. Garnish with chopped chives.

Recommended wines: *Ehrenfelser, Gewürztraminer*

Warm Potato and Mussel Salad
Serves 8

Nancy Carlman won the 1991 Penn Cove Mussel Recipe Contest, which is hosted each year by the Captain Whidbey Inn, with this delicious salad recipe. (Serve it as a first course or a light lunch.)

Built entirely out of local Madrona logs, the Captain Whidbey Inn on Whidbey Island overlooks the shores of Penn Cove, where some of the world's tastiest mussels are raised.

  3 *pounds small (2-inch) mussels, scrubbed*
  ½ *cup dry white wine*
  2 *shallots, minced*
  2 *pounds small new potatoes, in their skins*

French Dressing
  ¼ *cup white wine vinegar*
  ½ *cup olive oil*
  Salt
  Freshly ground black pepper
  Pinch of dry mustard

Garnish
  1 *tablespoon minced fresh parsley*
  1 *tablespoon minced fresh chives*

Place the mussels, wine, and shallots in a large cooking pot. Cover and cook over high heat for about 6 minutes, or until the mussels have opened. Remove from the heat. When cool enough to handle, remove the mussels from their shells and discard the shells.

Place the potatoes in a large pot with water to cover. Bring to a boil and cook until just tender, about 15 minutes. Drain.

While they are still warm, slice the potatoes ¼ inch thick. Combine the mussels and the potatoes in a salad bowl.

In a small bowl, combine the dressing ingredients and pour over the salad. Garnish with parsley and chives and serve warm.

Recommended wines: *Pinot Blanc, Fumé Blanc, young fruity Pinot Noir, champagne*

Old-Fashioned Cocktail Sauce
Makes 1½ cups

Chris Keff of the Sheraton Hotel's Hunt Club restaurant in Seattle, Washington, concocted this peppery sauce to serve over fresh snow crab or tanner crab legs. The snow crab is a long-legged spider crab with very sweet meat that is found in the north Pacific, mainly off Alaska in the Bering Sea and north of the Bering Strait. Snow crab is very perishable and is usually frozen immediately after processing. Much of the snow crab harvested in the Northwest is shipped to Japan, where it has been popular for many years.

  2 *pounds tomatoes (4 medium), cored*
  1 *tablespoon salt*
  ½ *tablespoon mustard seed*
  ¼ *tablespoon whole allspice*
  ¼ *tablespoon black peppercorns*
  2 *tablespoons chopped shallots*
  1 *garlic clove, minced*
  1 *tablespoon grated fresh gingerroot*
  1 *teaspoon red pepper flakes*
  ¼ *cup white wine vinegar*
  ¼ *cup grated fresh horseradish or ¼ cup prepared horseradish*

Quarter the tomatoes and place them in a heavy-bottomed, noncorrosive saucepan. Sprinkle the tomatoes with the salt and cook them over medium heat for about 7 minutes, or until they begin to release their juices.

Grind the mustard seed, allspice, and black peppercorns together in a mortar or food processor. Add the ground spices to the tomatoes. Next stir in the shallots, garlic, ginger, red pepper, and vinegar.

Simmer the sauce over low heat until it is thickened, about 20 minutes, stirring occasionally. Add the grated horseradish and chill. Serve with fresh crab or shrimp.

Recommended wine: *Sauvignon Blanc*

Panfried Oysters Parmesan
Serves 2

Fred Carlo, the owner of Salumeria di Carlo in Portland, Oregon, is best known for making exceptional sausages, pepperoni, and prosciutto at his Italian-style deli. In this fantastic oyster recipe, he dips freshly shucked oysters into a batter of egg, grated Parmesan cheese, and chopped parsley, then sautés them to a crisp golden brown. Homemade tartar sauce seasoned with lemon juice and capers is the perfect counterpoint.

24 small or medium freshly shucked oysters
2 large eggs
½ cup grated Parmesan or Romano cheese
1 tablespoon minced fresh parsley or cilantro
¼ teaspoon freshly ground black pepper
¼ cup vegetable oil
   Tartar sauce, preferably homemade
   Hot red pepper sauce
   Lemon wedges

Drain the oysters of their liquor and reserve for another use if desired. In a small mixing bowl, whisk together the eggs, grated cheese, parsley, and pepper. Heat the vegetable oil in a heavy-bottomed skillet over medium heat until a tiny bit of egg batter dropped into the oil sizzles.

Dip each oyster into the egg batter and gently place in the hot oil. Line the bottom of the skillet, leaving plenty of space between the oysters. (Cook the oysters in batches.) Cook the oysters until golden brown, turning once, about 1½ minutes per side. Drain the oysters on paper towels.

Serve warm with tartar sauce, red pepper sauce, and lemon.

Recommended wines: *Pinot Gris, Fumé Blanc*

Grilled Oysters with Rhubarb-Ginger Compote
Serves 4

"Oysters taste of the briny sea and they have an earthy freshness that marries beautifully with the tartness of rhubarb in this rhubarb-ginger compote," says British Columbian cooking-show host and producer Gary Faessler.

Compote
2 rhubarb stalks, thinly sliced
1 shallot, minced
1 teaspoon grated fresh gingerroot
2 tablespoons mirin (Japanese sweet cooking wine) or sherry
   Juice of ½ lime
2 tablespoons white wine

12 freshly shucked oysters
1 tablespoon olive oil or unsalted butter, melted

Combine all the compote ingredients in a nonreactive saucepan. Cook over medium heat, stirring often, until the rhubarb has softened and the compote has a thick, saucelike consistency. Set aside.

Brush the oysters lightly with the olive oil or melted butter and grill them over a hot flame for about 3 minutes on each side, or until the oysters are just heated through.

To serve, spoon some of the compote onto each plate and arrange 3 oysters in the center.

Recommended wines: *Dry rhubarb wine, champagne*

Above: **Oysterman Dan Driscoll and Jeanne Skott grill freshly harvested Willapa Bay oysters.**

Grilled Oysters (Bachelor's Barbecue)

One of oysterman Dan Driscoll's favorite ways to cook oysters is to barbecue them over hot coals until they open—a dish he calls "Bachelor's Barbecue." He also steams oysters with clams over sake and serves the nectar along with the shellfish (page 32).

When cooked in their shells over a fire oysters develop a flavor more complex than a great Burgundy, with hints of mushrooms, truffles, smoke, and earth. Serve these as an appetizer to accompany grilled steak and a tossed green salad.

1 dozen oysters per person, in the shell

Preheat a grill or barbecue and position the grill about 6 inches above the coals. Place the oysters, deep side down, over the hot coals. Cook just until the oysters open, about 13 to 15 minutes. Serve warm.

Recommended wines: *Semillon-Sauvignon Blanc, Chardonnay, Pinot Gris*

Scalloped Oysters
Serves 4

Dolores Husted lives on a ranch in Montana's "Big Hole" country. She loves this creamy oyster dish for family gatherings.

> $1\frac{1}{2}$ *cups crushed saltine crackers*
> 2 *pints small oysters in their liquor*
> 4 *tablespoons ($\frac{1}{2}$ stick) unsalted butter*
> 1 *cup half-and-half*
> $\frac{1}{4}$ *cup dry sherry (optional)*

Preheat the oven to 350° F.

Lightly grease a 2-quart casserole dish. Sprinkle $\frac{1}{2}$ cup cracker crumbs over the bottom of the dish and top with half of the oysters and their liquor. Dot the oysters with one-third of the butter and pour $\frac{1}{2}$ cup of the half-and-half over them.

Add another layer of cracker crumbs, oysters, butter, and half-and-half. Sprinkle the sherry with the remaining cracker crumbs and butter. Bake for about 30 minutes, or until golden.

Recommended wines: *Chenin Blanc (Melon)*

DuPuis Pink Sauce for Cracked Dungeness Crab
Makes 2 cups

This recipe was originally published in *The Ford Treasury of Favorite Recipes from Favorite Eating Places* in 1950, when the DuPuis Seafood Inn in Port Angeles, Washington, was run by Mrs. Karl Kirk. Lori's grandmother was a DuPuis and she adopted this recipe as though it had been passed down from her own mother. Her family never had cracked crab without it. Store, covered, in the refrigerator up to 3 days.

1 cup mayonnaise
1 cup red chili sauce
1 teaspoon Worcestershire sauce
2 teaspoons horseradish
4 sweet pickles, chopped fine
2 celery stalks
4 green onions
4 parsley sprigs
1 tablespoon sugar

Combine all of the ingredients together in a medium bowl until well mixed. Serve with cracked Dungeness crab.

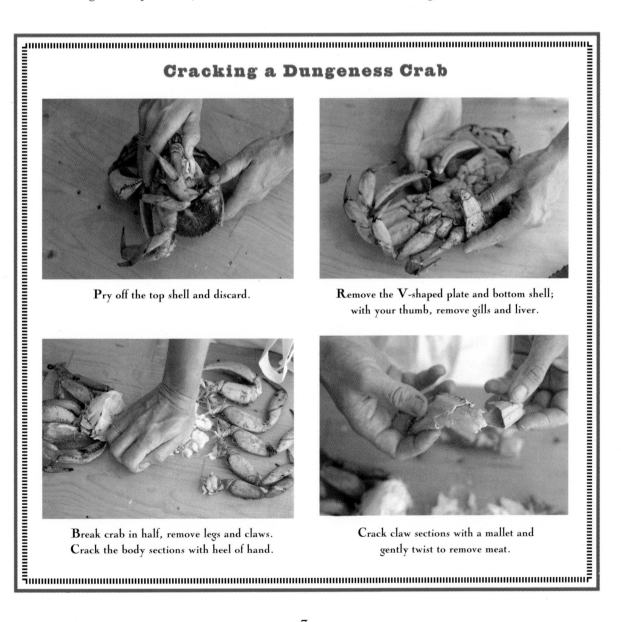

Cracking a Dungeness Crab

Pry off the top shell and discard.

Remove the V-shaped plate and bottom shell; with your thumb, remove gills and liver.

Break crab in half, remove legs and claws. Crack the body sections with heel of hand.

Crack claw sections with a mallet and gently twist to remove meat.

Sake-Steamed Oysters and Clams
Serves 2

During the winter months, when low tides tend to occur at night, oysterman Dan Driscoll from Oysterville Sea Farms, on the Long Beach Peninsula in Washington, often works his oyster and clam beds under less than desirable weather conditions. He discovered the perfect antidote to biting-cold winds and driving rain with this dish of oysters and clams steamed over sake. After steaming the shellfish, he pours the hot sake-infused nectar into a mug and drinks it along with the dish.

> 1½ *cups sake*
> 2 *dozen small oysters in the shell, scrubbed*
> 2 *dozen small steamer clams in the shell, scrubbed*
>
> 1 *garlic clove, minced*
> 4 *tablespoons (½ stick) unsalted butter, melted*
> *Lemon slices*

Pour the sake into the bottom of a 2-quart steamer or a large saucepan fitted with a steamer basket. Place the oysters in a layer on the bottom of the steamer basket and place the clams on top of the oysters.

Cover and bring the sake to a boil, then reduce the heat and simmer for about 10 minutes, or until the clams have popped open. (The oysters will open slightly or not at all.) Discard any clams that do not open. Dish the oysters and clams into 2 bowls and strain the steaming liquid into 2 large mugs.

Combine the minced garlic and melted butter and serve in side dishes for dipping, along with the lemon slices. To open the oysters, insert an oyster or paring knife at the ruffled end and twist to pry open.

Recommended beverage: *Beer or ale*

Plackie Sturgeon
Serves 4 to 6

Brian Davis, a Columbia River fisherman from the historic fishing community of Clifton, Oregon, has earned kudos for his method of preparing "Plackie" sturgeon or salmon, a recipe taught to him by the Greek fishermen who once inhabited Clifton. The dish combines fresh fish with spinach, green peppers, and carrots in tomato sauce. If he's lucky enough to have leftovers, Brian serves them over spaghetti.

> 1 *tablespoon olive oil*
> 1 *onion, diced*
> 3 *garlic cloves, minced*
> 1 *15-ounce can tomato sauce*
> ½ *cup water*
> 1 *15-ounce can stewed tomatoes*
> 1 *bunch fresh spinach, washed and chopped*
> 2 *large carrots, diced*
> 1 *green pepper, diced*
> 1½ *cups dry red wine*
> 1 *whole sturgeon or small salmon, about 2 pounds, cleaned*
> *Salt and black pepper to taste*

Heat the olive oil in a large skillet over medium heat. Sauté the onion and the garlic until they become transparent, about 5 minutes. Stir in the tomato sauce, water, and stewed tomatoes, then add the spinach, carrots, green pepper, and the red wine. Bring to a boil, then reduce the heat and simmer for about ½ hour, stirring occasionally.

Preheat the oven to 350° F.

Sprinkle the sturgeon with salt and pepper and place it in a large baking dish. Pour the hot sauce over the fish. Bake for about an hour, or until the backbone of the fish lifts out easily. Spoon a portion of fish and sauce onto each serving plate.

Recommended beverage: *Pinot Gris, Sauvignon Blanc*

Sautéed Abalone with Pink Gooseberry Sauce
Serves 4 as an appetizer

The sweet, delicately flavored meat of abalone, a large sea snail, was a favorite food of native North Coast Indians. Abalone are abundant in the waters off the west coast of Vancouver Island, where Sooke Harbour House owner Sinclair Philip often collects them while scuba diving. He serves abalone in a tart gooseberry sauce.

    12 ounces fresh or frozen abalone meat
    3   cups pink gooseberries (green may be
          substituted)
    ¾   cup Ehrenfelser or Riesling wine, plus 8
          tablespoons additional wine if needed
          for gooseberries
    8   tablespoons (1 stick) unsalted butter,
          chilled
    2   tablespoons unsalted butter

Slice the abalone into ¹⁄₁₆-inch slices and set aside. (If the meat has been freshly shucked, allow it to rest 15 minutes before slicing).

Puree the gooseberries in a food processor or blender, adding white wine if neccessary. Strain the puree through a sieve into a heavy-bottomed saucepan, and, stirring in the ¾ cup wine, bring the mixture to a boil. Reduce the heat and simmer the sauce for about 5 minutes, or until slightly thickened. Whisk in 6 tablespoons of butter, one tablespoon at a time. Remove the sauce from the heat and keep warm.

Melt the remaining 2 tablespoons of butter in a frying pan over high heat. Sauté the sliced abalone very quickly, for about thirty seconds, or until just heated through.

Pour the warm gooseberry sauce in a ring on a large preheated plate. Spoon the abalone into the center of the plate.

Recommended wine: Ehrenfelser or Riesling

Spicy Steamed Mussels
Serves 4

Lori's not sure where this recipe originated; she got it from her friend Camilla Bayliss, who got it from her friend Violetta, and it's wonderful. It combines sea-sweet mussels with hot chiles, fresh ginger, coriander, garlic, and other Asian spices to create a fiery appetizer; served over white rice it's also a great entrée.

    24 2-inch mussels
    3   tablespoons peanut oil
    2   large onions, finely chopped
    4   garlic cloves, minced
    1   inch-long piece fresh gingerroot, grated
    2   fresh hot red chiles (cayenne), seeded
          and diced
    ½   teaspoon ground turmeric
    3   teaspoons ground coriander
    ½   teaspoon salt
    1   cup water
    1   tablespoon chopped fresh coriander
          leaves
        Lime or lemon juice

Scrub the mussels well and set aside. Heat the oil in a wok or a large, deep saucepan over medium-high heat. Add the onions, garlic, and ginger and sauté until the onions are soft and golden, about 5 minutes. Add the chiles, turmeric, and coriander and continue to cook for about 3 minutes. Add the salt and water and bring the mixture to a boil, then reduce the heat and simmer for 5 minutes. Add the mussels, cover, and steam until the shells have opened, about 7 minutes, discarding any that do not open. Remove from the heat and sprinkle with the coriander. Add lime juice and salt to taste. Spoon the sauce over the mussels and into the shells and serve immediately.

Recommended wines: Sauvignon Blanc, Pinot Gris

Lemon-Pepper Razor Clams
Serves 4

Contrary to common practice, John Kroft believes that pounding razor clam meat before cooking it toughens rather than softens the meat. His melt-in-your-mouth tender razor clams are proof of his theory.

According to John, the key to his recipe is fresh clams. "When you dig the clams yourself you know they're absolutely fresh," he says. When he buys clams at a fish market, he checks for freshness by smelling the clams and by inspecting their color. If the clams emit a fishy odor or if the flesh is not creamy white, he won't buy them. Cook these clams to order—2 per serving.

> 2 *large eggs*
> ¼ *teaspoon freshly ground black pepper*
> ¼ *teaspoon salt*
> 8 *fresh razor clams, cleaned and blotted dry*
> 2 *tablespoons olive oil*
> 1 *tablespoon unsalted butter*
> 1 *teaspoon lemon pepper, or to taste*

Whisk the eggs, black pepper, and salt together in a mixing bowl. Dip each razor clam into the egg mixture, coating both sides of the clam thoroughly. Leave the clams in the egg mixture until needed.

Combine the olive oil and butter in a heavy-bottomed skillet and place the pan over medium-high heat until the butter sizzles. With a fork, stab the neck end of 2 clams and place the clams, front side down, in the frying pan (the back side has the hinge).

Sprinkle them lightly with lemon pepper and cook until the clams are lightly golden on the edges, about 1 to 2 minutes. Refrain from stirring the clams as they will lose their coating. Flip the clams and sprinkle them again with lemon pepper. Cook another 1 to 2 minutes, or until the clams are golden brown.

Dedicated clammers try to hit the beach before the tide turns, which means rising before dawn.

June's son, John Kroft, relaxes after a successful clamming expedition.

34

Razor Clamming

A warm fire in June Kroft's cozy beach cottage takes the chill off after an early morning clamming expedition. *Pictured:* Lemon-Pepper Razor Clams with Oven-Roasted Potatoes.

A MINUS TIDE ON THE NORTHWEST coast often rings clammers out in droves. Dressed in clamming gear—rubber boots or hip waders, sweatshirts and raingear, with gunnysack collecting bags tied to their belts—they line up along the seashore.

Performing a frenetic tribal warlike dance, they stomp and prance in circles around their territory, trying to rouse the dormant clams from their hiding places deep under the sand. A navel-shaped mark left on the sand's surface is the only indication as to where the clams are buried.

"The clams usually show twice—once before the tide turns and then again a bit later," explains June Kroft, an avid clammer who lives on the Oregon coast. "When they dig, the clams always head toward the sea," she says, positioning her shovel at a forty-five-degree angle northwest of a clam hole. Quickly and efficiently June digs a deep, straight hole, using the suction created by the draw of her shovel to pull the clam out. She seems to sense just how deep the hole should be and, once it is deep enough, she drops to her hands and knees. Her gentle face beams with excitement as she reaches in at arm's length and pulls out a long, fat razor clam.

Salmon with Blackberry-Pinot Noir Sauce
Serves 4

While picking blackberries along the water-front in Vancouver, British Columbia, tele-vision cooking-show host Gary Faessler noticed that just out from shore fishermen were catching fresh Coho salmon. Working spontaneously on the theme of fresh salmon and blackberries, he developed this recipe.

> 2 cups Fish Stock (page 21)
> 2 cups Pinot Noir or other dry red wine
> 2 shallots, minced
> 2 garlic cloves, minced
> 2 tablespoons fresh lemon thyme, minced
> ½ cup (1 stick) unsalted butter, chilled and cut into ½-inch cubes
> 4 dozen blackberries, about 2 cups
>
> 4 6-ounce fresh salmon fillets, boned
>
> Yellow nasturtium flowers for garnish (optional)

Combine the fish stock, wine, shallots, garlic, and thyme in a medium saucepan. Bring the mixture to a boil and cook over high heat until reduced to a syrup-like con-sistency, about 12 minutes.

Remove the pan from the heat and slow-ly whisk in the butter, bit by bit. Add the blackberries and heat the sauce through over low heat. Set aside and keep warm.

Steam the salmon fillets in a covered steamer over medium heat for 5 to 6 min-utes (depending on thickness), until the salmon is firm and barely pink in the center. Blot the salmon dry on paper towels. Spoon some of the blackberry sauce onto each plate and place a salmon fillet alongside the sauce. Garnish with nasturtium blossoms, if desired.

Recommended wine: *Pinot Noir*

Salmon Loaf with Lemon and Parsley Sauce
Serves 4 to 6

Whenever Lori's family returned to Seattle following a salmon fishing trip, they'd barbe-cue or oven bake the salmon the first night, then use the leftovers in this moist salmon loaf, which has always been a favorite of hers. This also makes great sandwiches.

> 1 cup bread crumbs
> ¾ cup milk
> ½ teaspoon salt
> 2 tablespoons finely chopped onion
> 2 tablespoons unsalted butter, melted
> 2 eggs, slightly beaten
> 2 cups flaked cooked salmon
> 3 tablespoons fresh lemon juice
> ½ teaspoon pepper
> 2 tablespoons finely chopped celery
> ⅛ teaspoon grated nutmeg
>
> **Lemon and Parsley Sauce**
> ½ cup (1 stick) unsalted butter
> ⅛ teaspoon salt
> 2 tablespoons minced fresh parsley
> ¼ cup fresh lemon juice

Preheat the oven to 350° F.

In a large mixing bowl, combine the ingredients for the salmon loaf in the order given, mixing well. Oil a loaf pan and press the mixture into the pan. Bake about 40 minutes, or until a knife inserted in the center comes out clean.

While the salmon loaf is baking, prepare the sauce: Melt the butter over medium heat in a saucepan. Whisk in the remain-ing ingredients. Serve hot over slices of salmon loaf.

Recommended wines: *Sauvignon Blanc (Fumé Blanc), Pinot Gris*

Grilled Swordfish with Moroccan Chermoula
Serves 6

At Zefiro Restaurant in Portland, Oregon, Chef Chris Israel serves this spicy dish with couscous and grilled vegetables.

Chermoula
    5 garlic cloves, minced
    1 bunch of fresh cilantro, chopped
 1/2 cup chopped fresh parsley
    1 tablespoon paprika
    1 tablespoon toasted cumin seeds, ground,
         or 1 tablespoon ground cumin, toasted
 1/2 teaspoon cayenne pepper
       Juice of 3 lemons
 3/4 cup extra virgin olive oil
       Salt, to taste

    6 6-ounce center-cut swordfish steaks

Combine all the *chermoula* ingredients in a large nonreactive bowl; set aside 1/4 cup.

Place the swordfish in the remaining *chermoula* sauce and turn to cover on both sides. Cover and marinate in the refrigerator for 4 hours or overnight. Remove the fish from the marinade and grill over charcoal or hardwood, or broil, turning once, until it has just cooked through, about 5 minutes per side.

Transfer the swordfish to warm plates and top with the *chermoula*.

Recommended wines: *Pinot Noir, Nebbiolo, Chardonnay*

Smoked Black Cod in Ginger Broth
Serves 4

Freshly smoked black cod, or sablefish, has an incredible silky texture and rich smoky flavor. Chef Rob Pounding of the Salishan Lodge on the Oregon coast serves it in a shimmering copper-colored, ginger-infused broth surrounded with colorful diced vegetables. It's a sensational combination of flavors and textures.

    3 cups chicken stock
    3 cups Fish Stock (page 21) or bottled
         clam juice
 1/4 cup chopped lemongrass
    2 tablespoons grated fresh gingerroot
 1/2 cup finely diced shiitake mushrooms
 1/2 cup finely diced yellow squash
 1/2 cup finely diced carrots
 1/2 cup peeled and finely diced cucumber
  12 ounces freshly smoked black cod
         (sablefish)

Combine the chicken and fish stocks in a large kettle.

Place the lemongrass and ginger in a tea strainer or tie them in a square of cheesecloth and place in the stock. Simmer the stock over medium heat for about 15 minutes; discard the seasonings. Add the vegetables and cook until tender, about 5 minutes.

Preheat the broiler. Broil the cod about 2 minutes on each side, just enough to heat through. Remove any skin from the fish and divide into 4 portions; remove and discard any bones.

Place each serving of fish in a warmed soup bowl and ladle hot broth over the cod. Divide the vegetables evenly among the bowls and serve immediately.

Recommended wines: *Chardonnay, Semillon-Sauvignon Blanc, dry Riesling*

Grilled Picnic Salmon with Peachy Barbecue Sauce
Serves 12

Fresh Chinook salmon from the Columbia River has a delicate fruity flavor reminiscent of fresh peaches that is deliciously highlighted by this tangy barbecue sauce made with peach preserves. This recipe makes enough to feed twelve hungry people, but it can easily be adapted for a smaller portion of salmon.

Peachy Barbecue Sauce
½ cup (1 stick) unsalted butter
1 red onion, minced
4 garlic cloves, minced
½ cup soy sauce
1 tablespoon Dijon mustard
½ cup firmly packed brown sugar
½ cup fresh lemon juice
1 cup peach preserves
½ cup red wine vinegar

1 10-pound salmon fillet

½ cup chopped fresh chives, for garnish

Combine all the ingredients for the barbecue sauce in a large saucepan. Bring to a boil; reduce the heat and simmer for ½ hour, or until slightly thickened. Set aside half the sauce for serving.

Preheat a charcoal grill. Make a sturdy foil pan large enough to hold the salmon fillet. Lay the salmon in the foil, skin side down. Brush the fish generously with the barbecue sauce. Set the foil pan containing the fish on the grill over medium-hot coals and grill, brushing occasionally with the sauce, for about 40 minutes, or until the salmon is firm to the touch. Garnish the salmon with fresh chives and pass extra sauce separately.

Recommended wines: *Pinot Noir, Pinot Gris*

Opposite: **A** peach-based barbecue sauce heightens the natural sweetness of fresh salmon. *Above:* **A** twist on the standard **Bloody Mary**.

Clamato Bloody Mary
Makes one drink

After a morning of razor clamming, the Kroft family fills a big bowl full of tangy Bloody Marys made with Clamato juice and sips them while cleaning and cooking their clams. In Canada, this popular drink is called a "Caesar."

1½ ounces vodka
5 ounces Clamato juice
Several drops Worchestershire sauce to taste
Salt and freshly ground pepper to taste
Fresh lime or lemon slices
Celery stalks for garnish

Combine the vodka, Clamato juice, Worchestershire sauce, and tabasco sauce, mixing well. Season to taste with salt and pepper. Pour over ice into tall glasses and top with lemon slices. Garnish with celery stalks.

Pasta with Northwest Pesto and Spot Shrimp
Serves 2

Jeanne Skott makes pesto ahead and freezes it or stores it in the refrigerator until she's ready to cook. Then she tosses it together with pasta and shrimp, which she boils in seawater, for a quick, easy meal. The difference between shrimp and prawns is that shrimp are taken from salt water, prawns from fresh water. Both are excellent in this dish.

> 2   *quarts fresh seawater or 2 quarts water plus 2 tablespoons salt*
> 1   *pound whole shrimp (shells on)*
> 8   *ounces linguine or spaghetti*

In a large pot, bring the salted water to a boil over high heat. Drop the shrimp into the boiling water and cook until pink. Small shrimp will be done almost immediately, and larger ones will need to cook ½ to 1 minute. Drain the shrimp, and when they are cool to the touch, remove the shells and devein them.

Meanwhile bring another large pot of salted water to a boil. Add the pasta and cook just until al dente; drain and place in a large bowl.

Add ½ cup Jeanne's Northwest Pesto and toss. Add the cooked shrimp and serve.
Recommended wines: *Pinot Gris, Pinot Blanc, Sauvingon Blanc*

Jeanne's Northwest Pesto
Makes 2 cups

> ½   *cup hazelnuts*
> 5   *garlic cloves*
> 1   *teaspoon salt*
> ½   *teaspoon freshly ground black pepper*
> 4   *cups lightly packed fresh basil leaves*
> ½   *cup minced fresh parsley*
> 4   *ounces freshly grated Parmesan cheese*
> 4   *ounces freshly grated Pecorino or Romano cheese*
> 2   *cups olive oil*

Grind the nuts in a food processor or blender to make a coarse meal. Add the garlic and salt and pepper; process to chop well. Set this mixture aside. Place the basil and parsley in the food processor and pulverize. With the processor on low speed, slowly add the olive oil, pushing ingredients into the center of the blade with a spatula as necessary. Add the cheeses and nut/garlic mixture, and blend until smooth.

Pack the pesto into a glass or plastic container, top with a layer of olive oil, and freeze up to six months, or store in the refrigerator up to 3 weeks.

Oven-Roasted Potatoes with Garlic and Basil
Serves 4 to 6

Leslie Sear prepares these savory potatoes to accompany her brother's Lemon-Pepper Razor Clams (page 34). They're also delicious with lamb, fish, or omelets.

> 10   *red-skinned new potatoes, quartered lengthwise*
> 2   *to 3 tablespoons olive oil*
> 3   *shallots, finely chopped*
> ½   *teaspoon lemon pepper*
> ½   *teaspoon dried basil*
> ¼   *teaspoon salt*
> 3   *garlic cloves, minced*

Oysterville Sea Farms

"WHEN IN HONOLULU BUY A PINEAPPLE. When in Oysterville buy oysters," say the handpainted signs outside Oysterville Sea Farms. Located on the four-mile-wide Long Beach Peninsula in southwest Washington, which is bounded by the Pacific Ocean to the west and Willapa Bay to the east, Oysterville is one of the oldest towns in Washington State. Long before the coming of white men to the area, native Chinook Indians harvested native Olympia oysters from Willapa Bay and dried or smoked them for later use.

Legend holds that in 1854, at the request of early settlers R. H. Espy and I. A. Clark, Chief Nahcati of the local native tribe directed the white men to the location of the native oyster beds. Espy and Clark crossed the bay by canoe through heavy fog and, by pounding on a hollow log, Chief Nahcati directed them to the oysters.

Realizing the significance of their find, Espy and Clark quickly filed Donation Land Claims and soon started shuttling canoeloads of oysters across the bay for shipment to San Francisco.

Today, Oysterville Sea Farms is Oysterville's last operating oyster farm and the only fishery building in Washington State to be listed on the National Register of Historic Buildings. "I'm trying to revive a dead industry here," says third-generation oysterman Dan Driscoll. "I want to provide a link to Oysterville's past by reviving the oyster industry here."

Driscoll raises Pacific oysters and a variety of steamer clams, including Manila clams, native littlenecks, and cherrystones. He harvests just enough to sell in one day, returning any he doesn't sell are returned to the bay. Though time consuming, this practice guarantees absolute freshness and quality.

Oysterville Sea Farm's retail store is located in the old cannery built right on the shores of Willapa Bay. A twenty-foot-long cement table located just inside the cannery was built for shucking oysters back in 1939, and now serves as a workspace for sorting oysters and clams. From the old cannery one can see up and down Willapa Bay.

In the Pacific Northwest there are four main varieties of oysters in cultivation. These include the tiny native Olympia oyster (Ostrea lurida); the Pacific oyster (Crassostrea gigas), a native of China and Japan, which was introduced to the States in the 1920s; the Belon or European flat oyster (Ostrea edulis); and the Kumamoto (Crassostrea sikamea), a small variety of Pacific oyster.

Depending on where they are grown and on different varieties, oysters can taste of salty brine, of the cold slap of the sea, of fog, kelp, iodine, flinty minerals, cucumbers, mushrooms, egg yolk, or tapioca. Factors that can affect their color, shape, and flavor include water salinity levels, the presence of algae or eel grass in the growing beds, soil, rainfall, and different growing methods (bottom culture, raft or tray culture, and dike culture are some of the methods used).

Preheat the oven to 350° F.

Arrange the potatoes in a shallow roasting pan in a single layer; do not overcrowd the pan or the potatoes will steam instead of browning. Sprinkle the olive oil evenly over the potatoes and distribute the shallots, lemon pepper, dried basil, and salt over them. Toss gently to distribute the herbs.

Bake the potatoes for about 30 minutes, then remove from the oven and turn the golden side under. Sprinkle the potatoes with the chopped garlic and return to the oven for about 20 minutes, or until they are a rich golden brown.

Blake Island Barbecue Sauce
for Salmon
Makes ³/₄ cup sauce

At Blake Island State Park, a 45-minute boat ride from Seattle, the native Indians still cook salmon the way their ancestors did. A whole salmon is split and cleaned then butterflied out and inserted between two upright poles, each about 5 feet in length, which are wired together at each end of the salmon. Thin cedar splints inserted horizontally across the front and back of the salmon keep it flat while cooking. The long poles are then stuck in the ground close to the hot embers, where the salmon cooks slowly. The poles can be turned toward or away from the fire to regulate the heat.

This is Lori's mother's version of the sauce they serve to accompany salmon at Blake Island. It's smoky and rich and is equally good with grilled or oven-baked salmon.

> 3 tablespoons Worcestershire sauce
> Grated rind and juice of 1 lemon
> ½ cup catsup
> 2 tablespoons unsalted butter
> 3 tablespoons brown sugar
> 2 tablespoons cider vinegar
> 2 teaspoons liquid smoke (optional)
> 1 medium onion, grated
> ½ teaspoon salt
> Few drops hot red pepper sauce

Combine all of the ingredients in a non-reactive saucepan and bring to a boil over medium-high heat. Serve warm as an accompaniment to grilled or baked salmon.

Wind-Dried Salmon

LLOYD AND IDA MARY LEY, members of the Seton Lake Band of the Lilloet Indians, live with their four children, Berry, Sherry, Storm, and Vision, near the Fraser River in southern British Columbia, Canada. Each summer when the sockeye salmon are running the family sets up camp under a yellow tarp along the river beneath a large sister pine tree. Here they fish for salmon, which they preserve by wind-drying, an ancient technique.

"People see the wind-dried salmon and it looks strange to them," says Lloyd, "but many other cultures, like the Chinese, have been wind-drying salmon and other fish for thousands of years."

The sockeye are fished by several different methods—with long-handled dip nets, with small gill nets (which fish selectively according to the size of the fish's gills), and by set nets, which, according to Ida Mary, look similar to a dip net but are held in place by ropes anchored to shore.

Once the salmon have been caught, Ida Mary removes the head and the fins and butterflies the salmon, slicing along first one side of the backbone, then the other. The backbone of the fish is removed, but the tail is kept intact.

She then cuts deep horizontal slits through the flesh, about 1½ inches apart, down the entire length of the fish. Next, grasping the fish firmly by its tail, she stretches it, separating the slices of meat, which are still attached to the skin. The salmon fillet is then rubbed with salt to discourage flies and hung to dry in the sun and wind for 2 weeks.

The dry, jerkylike flesh of the wind-dried salmon tastes of the dry parched wind off the river. "Wind-dried salmon is great to take along when you're hiking in the mountains," says Ida Mary. "It's very light to carry and it takes just a little bit of salmon to make a good soup."

Vividly hued wind-dried salmon fillets.

Lloyd Ley nets a glistening
sockeye salmon.

Ida Mary Ley slits the flesh to
facilitate drying.

The stretched fillet is salted and
hung to dry.

Leslie's
Rhubarb-Strawberry Pie
Serves 6 to 8 (one 9-inch pie)

This lattice-topped pie is a traditional finale to a razor clam brunch in the Kroft family.

1 *cup diced fresh or partially thawed*
   frozen strawberries
4 *cups diced rhubarb*
2 *teaspoons grated fresh lemon rind*
1 *tablespoon fresh lemon juice*
1 *cup sugar*
3 *tablespoons quick-cooking tapioca*
2 *tablespoons unsalted butter*
   Pastry for a 2-crust pie
1 *tablespoon milk or cream*

Preheat the oven to 400° F.

Combine the strawberries, rhubarb, lemon rind, lemon juice, sugar, and tapioca in a mixing bowl. Let the mixture sit for 15 to 20 minutes.

Roll one-half of the pastry out and line a 9-inch pie tin, letting the excess pastry hang over the edges of the pan. Spoon the fruit filling into the lined pie tin and dot with the butter.

Roll out the remaining pastry and cut it into 1-inch-wide strips. Weave the strips over the top of the pie in a crosswise pattern to create a lattice effect over the top of the pie. Trim and crimp the edges of the crust. Brush the top of the pastry with milk or cream and bake for 12 minutes, then reduce the heat to 350° F. and bake for 30 to 40 minutes more, or until the crust is browned and the filling is set. Serve the pie with whipped cream or ice cream.

Thimbleberry Cobbler
Serves 6

Thimbleberries (*Rubus parviflorus*) are shallow-cupped scarlet-colored berries with a very sweet maple-sugar flavor balanced by tart acids. They are indigenous to many parts of the Northwest coast and were often utilized by the native people of the area. Thimbleberries are very juicy and are best used as soon as possible after they are picked. They do not store well.

Raspberries or salmonberries, which are both closely related to thimbleberries, can also be used in this recipe.

4 *cups thimbleberries*
4 *tablespoons unbleached all-purpose*
   flour
2/3 *cup sugar*
Cream Biscuit Dough
2 *cups unbleached all-purpose flour*
1 *tablespoon baking powder*
1/2 *teaspoon salt*
1/4 *cup (1/2 stick) unsalted butter, chilled,*
   cut in pieces
3/4 *cup heavy cream*
2 *tablespoons sugar*

Combine the berries with the flour and sugar in a mixing bowl and mix gently. Turn the berries into an oiled baking dish or casserole dish with a 1-quart capacity.

Preheat the oven to 400° F.

Make the biscuit dough by sifting the flour, baking powder, and salt together in a mixing bowl. With a pastry cutter, cut the butter into the flour until it is reduced to 1/8-inch pieces. Quickly stir in the cream. As soon as a soft dough has formed, turn it out onto a lightly floured surface and knead very lightly, just enough to combine the ingredients thoroughly.

Pinch off tablespoon-size pieces of biscuit dough and distribute them evenly over the top of the berries. Sprinkle the top of the dish with sugar and bake for 20 to 25 minutes, or until the biscuits are golden brown. To double-check if the biscuits are done, gently lift one of the biscuits from the berries with a fork. If the biscuit is not thoroughly cooked underneath, return the cobbler to the oven and check every 5 minutes until completely cooked. Serve warm with heavy cream or ice cream.

Recommended wine: *Late harvest Riesling*

Chocolate-Cranberry Torte
Makes one 10-inch cake

Cranberries grow in flat boggy areas throughout the Northwest. Many of the areas where cranberries once grew wild are now cultivated and cranberries have become an important regional crop. Their tart refreshing flavor is especially fine when combined with rich bittersweet chocolate in this dense chocolate torte.

   12 *ounces (1 package) fresh or frozen*
          cranberries
    1 *cup water*
    2 *cups sugar*
   ¾ *cup (1½ sticks) unsalted butter,*
          softened
  1½ *cups sugar*
    6 *large eggs, at room temperature*
   12 *ounces bittersweet or semisweet*
          chocolate, melted
    2 *teaspoons vanilla extract*
  1½ *cups sifted all-purpose unbleached flour*
   ¾ *cup (6 ounces) ground almonds*
          Chocolate Glaze (recipe follows)

Combine the cranberries, water, and sugar in a saucepan and bring to a boil over medium-high heat. Cook, stirring often, just until the cranberries start to pop, about 10 minutes. Drain the cranberries in a sieve and let cool.

Meanwhile, cream the butter and sugar together in a mixing bowl until the mixture is light and fluffy. Add the eggs one at a time, mixing thoroughly after each addition. Mix in the chocolate, vanilla, and flour, beating until all the ingredients are well blended. Fold in the ground almonds.

Preheat the oven to 325° F.

Line a 10-inch springform pan with parchment paper or wax paper. Oil and flour the paper. Spread a 1-inch layer of chocolate batter to cover the bottom of the pan. Distribute the cranberries evenly over the batter, then top with the remaining batter. Bake the torte for about 40 minutes, or until a toothpick inserted in the center comes out clean. Cool the cake in the pan.

To serve, remove the sides from the pan and place the torte on a serving plage. sprinkle the torte with powdered sugar or cover with chocolate glaze.

Chocolate Glaze
Makes 1 cup

    8 *ounces bittersweet or semisweet*
          chocolate, broken
   ½ *cup heavy cream*

Combine the chocolate and the cream in the top of a double boiler and melt over medium heat, stirring often with a whisk.

Pour the warm glaze over the top of the cake and, using a long metal spatula, distribute the glaze evenly over the top and sides of the cake. Chill the cake or let it sit at room temperature until the glaze has set.

the
FARMLANDS

IKE MANY PEOPLE RAISED in the Pacific Northwest, my earliest memories of food revolve around farm-raised fruits and vegetables. As a child growing up in the Seattle area, I often accompanied my mother to her favorite garden market at the Overlake Blueberry Farm in Bellevue, where the scents, sounds, and sights of the lively market enveloped my senses. It was there that I learned the secrets of selecting produce—of picking only fruits and vegetables that sparkled with life, heavy with the sensual weight of ripeness, and that exuded the quintessential aroma produce exudes only when it has attained perfection.

Nothing is more fulfilling than tucking a tiny seed into the moist, rich earth and nurturing it as it develops into a healthy fruit or vegetable. At his home on Orcas Island, Michael and his family have come to rely on their garden for near year-round supplies of produce.

Located in the San Juan Islands north of Seattle, Orcas Island lies in a rain shadow of the Northwest known as the "banana belt," which receives less-than-average rainfall. This gives island dwellers a head start on the growing season. Honeybees buzz around the fragrant blossoms of the apricot tree at the head of Jeanne Skott's garden, and mounded rows, surrounded by a heavy mulch of hay, are lined with baby greens, radicchio, herbs, and strawberry vines interwoven with purple-spiked Egyptian onions.

When Michael and Jeanne first moved to Orcas Island, their waterfront property was completely overrun with twenty-foot-high blackberry vines. Among their first priorities was digging a garden, and now dinner is often based on what is fresh in the garden.

Farming is a way of life for many people in the Pacific Northwest. Crops, including corn, apples, pears, mint, hazelnuts, peaches, Walla Walla Sweet onions, walnuts, beans, onions, cabbage, and wine grapes, just to name a few, are raised throughout the countryside. Even within the Northwest's major metropolitan centers, backyards and inner-city community gardens teem with herbs, fruits, and vegetables.

Before the first pioneers began arriving in the Northwest in the early 1840s, Native Americans inhabited what are now the area's major agricultural regions, which stretch from the fertile river valleys and plains west of the Cascade Mountains to the arid sagebrush plateaus and prairies to the east. While the native Indians collected most of their food by hunting and gathering, they did practice some farming techniques, like the burning of camas and berry fields, which cleared the land of unwanted plants, encouraging certain crops to flourish.

The Indian women also harvested young tender shoots of cattails, fireweed, Indian celery, salmonberry, and blackberry and gathered wild nuts and acorns, the latter of which were packed in handwoven baskets and set in a cool running stream to remove their bitter flavor. Wild berries and fruits were gathered, including red and blue elderberries, currants, plums, rose hips, hawthorne, blackberries, huckleberries, salal, and soapberry, a transluscent red berry with a bittersweet flavor. Soapberries were often mashed, then whipped to a froth with a tree branch and eaten like ice cream for dessert.

Following six months of arduous travel from the east, early immigrants to the Northwest were forced to live off the land, much as the Native Americans did. Within a short time, however, determined pioneers had established homesteads, planted kitchen gardens, tilled and planted acres of farmland, and fenced in the open prairies to protect their growing herds of cattle and sheep, establishing what are now the Northwest farmlands.

Corn, still one of the Northwest's major crops, was one of the first planted. For many early families it was the staple food, if not the only food, and it was eaten fresh, canned, dried, or ground into meal. As many foods as possible were preserved for winter. Vegetables like green beans, pumpkins, and peas were dried in the sun or over a fire. Whole ripe tomatoes, watermelon, and other fruit were preserved in brine, and root vegetables, like carrots, turnips, and potatoes, were packed between layers of straw and stored in cool cellars dug in the damp earth. Fruits and berries were dried, cooked into jellies and jams, or made into juices and canned.

Within fifty years, Northwest growing regions were exporting produce on the competitive national market. Yellow Newton and Spitzenburg apples raised in Oregon's Hood River area, for example, were recognized as some of the best in the country. By the turn of the century, apple ranchers in the Wenatchee, Okanagan, and Yakima valleys were producing more apples than the old established fruit-growing states on the East Coast. Apples, pears, and other fruits were also raised successfully in other areas of central and western Oregon, central Washington, and the San Juan Islands.

Following the Civil War period, cattle and sheep ranching emerged as the main agricultural business in the Northwest, with the abundant bunch grass, duck grass, and blue grass of the open range feeding grounds providing ample food for cattle and sheep throughout much of the region. Dairy farming, too, prospered in many valleys in Oregon and Washington.

A variety of farm-raised edible flowers, including tuberous begonias and violets.

Above: Rural Northwestern farmlands often lie minutes away from metropolitan centers. *Right:* Rich volcanic soil, cool nights, and long summer days make Central Washington the "Apple Capital of the World."

Two breakfast favorites from **Northwest B & B's**: **Multigrain Waffles**, *above*, and **Lemon-Pecan Scones**, *opposite*.

Multigrain Waffles
Serves 8

Another winning breakfast offering from the Turtleback Farm Inn.

> 1 *cup unbleached all-purpose flour*
> 1 *cup whole wheat flour*
> 1 *cup buckwheat flour, oat flour, or cornmeal*
> 1 *tablespoon baking powder*
> ½ *teaspoon salt*
> ¾ *teaspoon baking soda*
> 1 *tablespoon sugar*
> 12 *tablespoons (1½ sticks) unsalted butter, melted and cooled*
> 3 *cups buttermilk*
> 6 *large eggs, separated*

Blend the flours, baking powder, salt, soda, and sugar thoroughly in a mixing bowl. In a large bowl, add the melted butter to the buttermilk. Whisk in the egg yolks and gradually whisk in the flour mixture.

Beat the egg whites until they are stiff but not dry; fold into the batter. Bake the batter by ⅓-cupfuls on a well-greased pre-heated waffle iron. Serve warm with honey or maple syrup.

Lemon-Pecan Scones
Makes 8 scones

Loragene Gaulin of the Roberts Creek Country Cottage Bed and Breakfast in British Columbia serves these lemony scones warm from the oven with lots of sweet butter and homemade blackberry jam.

> 2 *cups unbleached all-purpose flour*
> 4 *teaspoons baking powder*
> ½ *teaspoon salt*
> ½ *cup sugar*
> ¼ *cup (½ stick) unsalted butter, chilled*
> ¼ *cup chopped pecans*
> 1 *teaspoon finely grated lemon rind*
>   *Juice of 1 lemon*
> 1 *cup milk*

Preheat the oven to 425° F.

In a large mixing bowl, combine the flour, baking powder, salt, and sugar, mixing thoroughly. Cut in the butter until it is reduced to pea-size bits. Stir in the pecans and lemon rind. Stir in the lemon juice and milk. Knead the mixture lightly on a floured surface, adding more flour if the dough is too sticky.

Form the dough into a ball and place on a well-oiled cast-iron griddle or ovenproof skillet. Press down with the heel of your hand to flatten the dough into a circle about ¾ inch thick. Cut the circle into 8 wedges. Place the griddle or skillet in the oven and bake the scones for 15 to 20 minutes, or until golden brown. Serve warm.

Speckie Soup
Serves 2 to 4

When cold raindrops patter on the roof and drip off the eaves in a steady rhythm, Lori sometimes puts off the cold with Speckie Soup. Speckies is an Americanized word for German dumplings, or *spaetzle*. In the cooking process, something remarkable and unexpected happens to the simple ingredients. Potatoes, onion, bacon, and water are transformed into a creamy, savory broth.

The recipe for this soup has been handed down for generations in Lori's family, originating with her great-grandmother, "Mother D," who was born in Germany and later came to America. It was her grandfather's favorite dish.

2 *large russet potatoes*
6 *cups cold water*
4 *bacon slices, finely chopped*
1 *large onion, diced*
Speckies
2 *large eggs*
½ *teaspoon salt*
1 *cup unbleached all-purpose flour (approximately)*
Salt and black pepper to taste

Peel and dice the potatoes and place them in a large soup kettle. Cover the potatoes with the cold water and bring to a boil over medium-high heat. Reduce the heat and simmer until the potatoes are tender when pierced with a fork, 12 to 15 minutes.

While the potatoes are cooking, fry the bacon until crisp. Drain on paper towels and pour off all but 2 teaspoons of the bacon fat. Add the onion to the pan and sauté until softened, 5 to 6 minutes. Add the onion and bacon to the soup and simmer gently while you make the Speckies.

In a small bowl, mix the eggs with a fork to break up the yolks. Add the salt and enough flour to form a stiff dough. Using scissors or a knife dipped in flour, cut the dough into walnut-size pieces (about ½ inch thick), letting them drop into the simmering broth.

Simmer the soup for about 10 minutes, or until the Speckies are firm to the touch and rise to the surface. Season the soup with salt and pepper.

Recommended wine: *Pinot Noir*

Cream of Chestnut Soup
Serves 4 to 6

Although edible chestnuts are not native to the Northwest, stands of these magestic trees can be found on abandoned farms in the area; in fact, the two largest chestnut trees in the country can be found in Canby and Oregon City in Oregon. Several companies are now working to encourage the planting of more chestnut trees in the Northwest.

Compared to other nuts, chestnuts are surprisingly low in fat and protein content. Their sweet, starchy meat tastes more like a sweet potato than a nut.

1¼ *pounds chestnuts, roasted and peeled (see Note), or 1 pound prepared chestnut puree*
3 *cups chicken stock*
1½ *cups milk*
¼ *cup dry sherry*
1 *teaspoon crumbled tarragon leaves*
1 *garlic clove, minced*
Salt and white pepper to taste
½ *cup heavy cream*
Fresh tarragon leaves, for garnish (optional)

If using roasted chestnuts, place them in a large saucepan, cover with the chicken stock, and bring to a boil. Reduce the heat and simmer until the chestnuts are soft, about 20 minutes. Strain the chestnuts, reserving the stock.

Puree the chestnuts in a food processor

or blender, adding some of the milk if necessary to facilitate blending. Strain the chestnut puree through a fine sieve back into the soup kettle or add the puree if using prepared chestnut puree. Stir in the reserved chicken stock, milk, sherry, tarragon, and garlic and heat through. Season with salt and white pepper and stir in the heavy cream. Heat until hot, but do not allow the soup to boil. Serve in warm soup bowls and garnish with fresh tarragon leaves if desired.

Note: To roast chestnuts, make a crisscross incision on the flatter side of each nut with a sharp knife. Place the nuts in a pan in a preheated 375° F. oven and roast for about 15 minutes, or until the leathery shell and inner skin can easily be removed. Because the skins harden as the chestnuts cool, it is much easier to peel them while they are warm.

Recommended wines: *Dry sherry, Chardonnay*

Raven Hill Herb Farm's Chilled Sorrel and Spinach Soup
Serves 4

Spectacularly situated near the San Juan strait, with a breathtaking view of Mount Hood, Raven Hill Herb Farm is an herb lover's dream. Noel Richardson and Andrew Yeoman's thriving business supplies both herbs (and Noel's delicious recipes using herbs) to many professional kitchens throughout the Northwest. This tangy soup is cool and refreshing on a warm summer day.

4 cups (about 5 ounces) lightly packed sorrel leaves
4 cups (about 5 ounces) lightly packed spinach leaves
2 tablespoons unsalted butter
4 shallots, finely chopped
2 cups chicken stock
1½ cups half-and-half
Freshly ground black pepper

Cream Topping
½ cup plain yogurt
¼ cup heavy cream
Chive blossoms for garnish

Rinse the sorrel and spinach well under cold water. In a large saucepan, combine the sorrel and spinach and cook the greens in just the water that clings to their leaves over high heat until steam forms. Reduce the heat; cover and simmer until limp, about 4 minutes. Drain the greens and puree in a blender or food processor. Set aside.

Melt the butter in a large skillet and sauté the shallots for 3 to 4 minutes, or until soft and translucent. Stir in the chicken stock. Bring the mixture to a boil; reduce the heat and simmer for 5 minutes. Add the pureed greens to the stock, whisking constantly until smooth. Gradually whisk in the half-and-half. Season to taste with pepper. Puree the soup in a blender or food processor in two batches. Pour the soup into a nonreactive container, cover, and refrigerate until the soup is well chilled, at least eight hours or overnight.

To make the cream topping: Place the yogurt in a small bowl and gradually stir in the heavy cream. Stir the soup well, as it will separate during chilling, and pour into chilled soup bowls. Gently spoon the topping mixture over the soup and garnish with chive blossoms.

Recommended wines: *Sauvignon Blanc, Semillon*

Goat Cheese, Bacon, and Walla Walla Onion Frittata
Serves 4 to 6

Walla Walla onions, raised in eastern Washington, have a sweet, mild flavor that is often compared to that of Vidalia onions. They have a relatively short growing season, so don't hesitate to substitute other types of onions in this recipe.

> 3 bacon slices, diced
> 1 Walla Walla onion, sliced into
>   ¼-inch-thick rings
> 5 large eggs
> ¾ cup plain yogurt
> 5 ounces fresh goat cheese
> ¼ teaspoon white pepper
> 6 fresh whole sage leaves

Preheat the oven to 375° F.

Sauté the bacon in a skillet over medium heat until crisp. Drain the bacon on paper towels and reserve. Return the skillet to the heat, spooning out all but 1 teaspoon of the bacon grease. Add the onion rings and cook over medium heat, stirring often, for about 8 minutes, or until tender. Remove the skillet from the heat and set aside.

Oil a 2-quart soufflé dish or casserole dish. In a mixing bowl, whisk together the eggs and yogurt. Crumble the goat cheese into the egg mixture and mix thoroughly. Stir in the white pepper and turn the mixture into the prepared soufflé dish.

Distribute the bacon and sage leaves evenly over the top of the egg mixture. Spread the onion slices over the top, pressing them down lightly into the mixture.

Bake the frittata uncovered about 40 minutes, or until a knife inserted in the center comes out clean. Spoon onto serving plates.

Recommended wine: *Pinot Noir*

Sally Jackson Cheeses

THE ROAD LEADING to Sally Jackson's cheese farm just outside of Oroville, Washington, near the Canadian border, winds through golden pastures bordered with fire-red Sumac trees, white birch, and fragrant sagebrush. According to Sally, the cheeses she makes reflect the changes in season that her farm passes through each year. "Where the animals live and what they eat has a dramatic effect on the cheeses," she says. "In the summer months, when the animals are out to pasture, the milk is not as rich and the cheeses taste leaner."

Sally, who makes a variety of cheeses that she personally delivers to restaurants and retail cheese shops throughout the Seattle area, says she really didn't start learning about cheese making until she had developed a herd—a mixture of goats, sheep, and cows—and started making cheeses from their milk. Sally's herd is comprised of Nubian goats, which are prized for their extra-rich milk. "The walls at the dairy are full of the stuff that makes cheese," she says. "Everything is alive." Her products include both soft and hard goat cheeses, often flavored with ingredients like jalapeño pepper and garlic or dried tomatoes and oregano. Some of Sally's cheeses are also distributed as far away as New York markets.

At home, the Jacksons eat most of their cheese plain with bread or crackers, but many northwestern chefs, like Linda Shiosaki, formerly of Seattle's Alexis Hotel, often incorporate Sally's cheeses into their recipes. "We went through Sally's cheeses like great balls of fire," says Linda. "Her cheeses are absolutely wonderful."

Sally Jackson produces a variety of cheeses, including sheep milk cheese wrapped in chestnut leaves and cheeses rubbed with cocoa powder or wood ash, all traditional European methods of handling cheeses.

Oregon Blue Cheese Torte with Hazelnut Pastry

Serves 8 to 10

Many people in the Northwest feel that Thomas Vella's Oregon blue cheese from the Rogue River Valley in southern Oregon surpasses traditional French Roquefort. The cheese is creamier than a Danish blue, with a slight tang. Now in his late eighties, Thomas Vella arrived in Oregon in 1935 from his native Italy. "I came. I look around. I see the river running. I see the cow; she's-a-eating. It look good. I buy it," he says.

Serve this torte at room temperature as an appetizer with fresh fruit. It will keep in the refrigerator up to 3 days.

Hazelnut Pastry

½	cup hazelnuts, toasted and finely ground (page 82)
1	cup unbleached all-purpose flour
½	teaspoon salt
6	tablespoons unsalted butter, chilled, cut into small pieces
1	egg yolk
1	tablespoon dry red wine or cold water (approximately)

Blue Cheese Filling

4	ounces cream cheese, softened
½	cup plain yogurt
3	large eggs, separated
¼	teaspoon salt
¼	teaspoon black pepper
1	cup (4 ounces) crumbled Oregon blue cheese

Combine the hazelnuts, flour, and salt in a mixing bowl or food processor. Cut in the chilled butter until reduced to split pea–size pieces. Add the egg yolk and wine and blend to form a stiff dough. Form the pastry into a flat disk and let it sit about 10 minutes before rolling out. (At this point the pastry can be frozen or chilled. Bring to room temperature before using.)

Meanwhile, using an electric mixer, beat the cream cheese until smooth. Add the yogurt, beating at high speed until smooth. Add the egg yolks one at a time, beating well after each addition. Then beat in the salt and pepper.

Fold the crumbled blue cheese into the cream cheese mixture. Beat the egg whites with a pinch of salt until they form stiff peaks. Fold the whites into the cheese mixture.

Preheat the oven to 375° F.

Lightly grease the bottom of an 8½-inch springform pan or a 9-inch pie tin. Roll the pastry out to a circle about 12 inches in diameter. Line the pan, letting the extra pastry hang over the sides of the pan. Turn the filling into the pastry and fold the overhanging pastry back over the top of the filling. (The edges of the pastry will be ragged and the crust will not cover the top of the torte completely—this will create an appealing rustic look.) Sprinkle the top of the torte with freshly ground black pepper.

Bake the torte about 40 minutes, or until a knife inserted in the center comes out clean. Serve at room temperature.

Recommended wines: *Pinot Noir, Zinfandel*

Pear and Vanilla Bean Risotto
Serves 4

Delicately flavored with chicken broth, ripe
pears, and vanilla, this creamy risotto makes
a delicious side dish for chicken or poached
salmon.

> 2 tablespoons olive oil
> 1 cup Arborio rice
> 3 cups chicken broth
> ½ vanilla bean, split lengthwise
> ½ teaspoon salt
> 1 tablespoon sugar
> 1 ripe pear, peeled, cored, and diced

Heat the olive oil over medium-high heat
in a heavy-bottomed saucepan. Gradually
stir in the rice and stir for a minute or two.
Add the chicken broth, vanilla bean, salt,
and sugar. Bring the rice to a boil; reduce
the heat to a simmer and stir in the chopped
pear. Cover and cook about ½ hour, or
until the rice is tender.

Recommended wine: *Pinot Gris*

Peppered Potato Tart
Serves 4 to 6

Chef Kaspar Donier of Kaspar's by the Bay
in Seattle, Washington, serves this crispy
potato tart as a side dish for lamb, chicken,
or beef or as an appetizer with sausage, prosciutto, or grilled fish. Potatoes form the
crust and filling for this dish, which is low
in fat. The mashed and grated potatoes for
this recipe can be prepped up to 2 hours in
advance of serving.

> 2 pounds russet potatoes
> ½ teaspoon salt
> 2 tablespoons unsalted butter
> 3 tablespoons heavy cream
> Pinch of nutmeg
> ½ teaspoon coarsely ground black
> pepper
> 4 tablespoons olive oil
> Chopped fresh rosemary, to taste

Preheat the oven to 375° F.

Peel the potatoes. Cut half of the potatoes into 1-inch cubes; reserve the remaining potatoes in a bowl of cold water. Place
the cubed potatoes in a saucepan, season
with the salt, and cover with water. Boil
until very soft, about 20 minutes. Drain and
return the pan to low heat and allow the
potatoes to dry, approximately 2 minutes.
Add the butter, cream, nutmeg, and black
pepper, and mash the potatoes until smooth.
Cover and keep warm.

Shred the remaining potatoes with a
coarse cheese grater. Heat 2 tablespoons of
oil in a nonstick pan over medium heat until
a drop of water fizzles in the oil. Spread half
of the shredded potatoes in an approximate
8-inch circle in the pan and sauté for about
2 minutes, or until golden brown. Flip the
potato cake and brown on the other side for
about 2 more minutes. Once the potatoes
are crispy, remove them from the pan and
turn onto a plate. Repeat the process with
the remaining shredded potatoes, making 2
potato cakes or "crusts."

To assemble the tart, grease a baking
sheet. Place one shredded potato cake on
the bottom of the baking sheet. Top the
potato cake with mashed potatoes, sprinkle
with rosemary, and top with the second
potato cake.

Bake the tart for about 20 minutes, or
until crisp and heated through. Divide the
tart into wedges and serve hot.

Recommended wines: *Chardonnay, Pinot
Gris, Pinot Noir (depending on the main dish)*

Above: **Tricabbage slaw.** *Opposite:* **Pea Pod Salad.**

Farm-Style Cabbage Slaw

Serves 12

The flavor of this slaw really develops after chilling for at least 4 hours in the refrigerator. Because it makes a generous quantity, this is a terrific party dish.

 1 *head napa cabbage*
 1 *head savoy cabbage*
 1 *head purple cabbage*
 1 *tablespoon salt*
 1½ *cups mayonnaise*
 ½ *cup plain yogurt*
 1 *tablespoon caraway seeds*
 1 *tablespoon chopped fresh parsley*
 2 *garlic cloves, minced*
  Salt and freshly ground black pepper

Finely chop all the cabbages with a cleaver. Mix together in a large tub with the salt and let sit for ½ hour. Drain off any liquid that may have accumulated. Combine the remaining ingredients in a bowl, then fold into the chopped cabbage and season to taste. Chill 4 hours or overnight before serving.

Pea Pod Salad with Quillisascut Fennel Cheese

Serves 6

Fourth-generation cheese maker Lora Lea Misterly produces a variety of fresh and aged cheeses at her twenty-six-acre dairy in eastern Washington, including Spanish-style manchego and goat cheeses flavored with fennel, lavender, and dill.

 1 *pound sugar snap peas*
 6 *ounces Quillisascut fennel cheese or*
   plain goat cheese, crumbled
 10 *cherry tomatoes, halved*
 ¼ *cup minced red onion*
 1 *tablespoon chopped fresh basil*
 3 *tablespoons fruity olive oil*
 1 *tablespoon balsamic vinegar*
  Salt and freshly ground black pepper
  Fresh fennel sprigs for garnish

Tip and tail the snap peas and place in a bowl with the cheese, cherry tomatoes, onion, and basil. Whisk together the oil and vinegar and season to taste with salt and pepper. Toss the dressing together with the salad. Garnish with fresh fennel. Serve at room temperature or slightly chilled.

Beet and Potato Salad
Serves 6

This salad turns a beautiful brilliant red color after sitting for several hours. Prepare this at least 4 hours ahead or the night before.

1   red onion, finely chopped
4   medium yellow finn potatoes, cooked, peeled, and diced
2   medium beets, cooked, peeled, and diced
1   large dill pickle, minced
½   cup dill pickle juice
1   tablespoon sugar
1   garlic clove, crushed
½   cup mayonnaise
1   teaspoon celery seed
    Salt and freshly ground black pepper to taste
    Fresh dill sprigs, for garnish

Combine all the ingredients, except the fresh dill, in a large mixing bowl. Cover and let sit 4 hours or overnight in the refrigerator. Adjust the seasonings before serving and garnish with fresh dill.

Puree of Carrots with Cumin
Serves 8

In this recipe, Ron Zimmerman recommends using freshly ground cumin seed, which, he says, is far superior in flavor to store-bought ground cumin. He grinds his seed in a small mortar and pestle or in a clean pepper grinder. This looks especially nice served in individual ramekins.

2   tablespoons unsalted butter
2   shallots, minced
2   pounds carrots
2¼   cups water
2   teaspoons freshly ground cumin seed
2   teaspoons sugar
      Salt and white pepper to taste

Melt the butter in a large saucepan over medium heat. Sauté the shallots until tender, about 5 minutes. Rinse the carrots (it's not necessary to peel them) and slice into ½-inch-thick pieces. Add the carrots to the shallots along with the water, cumin, and sugar. Cook, uncovered, until the carrots are tender and the water has evaporated, about 15 to 20 minutes. (If necessary, drain any remaining water from the carrots.)

Puree the carrots in a food processor or blender until smooth. Press the puree through a medium-fine wire strainer. If necessary, thin slightly with a little milk or cream. Season with salt and pepper.

Note: The puree can be prepared a day ahead and reheated.

Pickled Dilled Beans
Makes 4 pints

These crisp beans are delicious served in place of celery sticks in Bloody Marys.

2   pounds fresh green beans
2   garlic cloves, halved
1   cup white vinegar
2   tablespoons pickling salt
2   teaspoons chopped fresh dill
¼   teaspoon cayenne pepper

Rinse and drain the green beans. Trim the ends and cut the beans to fit into pint canning jars with ½ inch of head space. Place the beans in a saucepan over medium-high heat and cover with boiling water; cook just until they are tender but still slightly crisp, about 3 minutes. Drain and pack lengthwise into 4 hot sterilized jars. Place ½ clove of garlic in each jar.

In a 4- to 6-quart kettle, combine the vinegar, 3 cups water, pickling salt, dill, and cayenne. Bring the mixture to a boil and pour over the beans, leaving ½-inch headspace. Screw on the lids and process in a boiling water bath for 10 minutes.

Baked Butternut Squash with Hazelnuts
Serves 6

Garam masala, an East Indian spice mixture that Shelburne Inn co-owner Laurie Anderson discovered while traveling, is available in specialty food stores and spice shops. If you can't locate *garam masala,* substitute curry powder. Laurie serves this dish to accompany her Cranberry Pot Roast (page 78), but it's also delicious with chicken or pork.

>   2 *butternut squash, halved lengthwise*
>   5 *tablespoons unsalted butter*
>   ¾ *teaspoon garam masala*
>   ½ *teaspoon salt*
>   ¼ *freshly ground black pepper*
>   ½ *cup chopped toasted hazelnuts*
>   *(see page 82)*

Preheat the oven to 375° F.

Bake the squash, cut side down, on a baking sheet for about 40 minutes, or until tender. Allow the squash to cool slightly, then use a spoon to scoop out the seeds and discard.

Scrape the squash flesh into a mixing bowl and mash with a potato masher. Add the butter, *garam masala,* salt, and pepper, mixing well. (At this point the squash mixture can be chilled for up to 2 days or set aside at room temperature for up to 2 hours, as needed.) To serve, reheat the squash in a medium saucepan over medium heat, stirring often. Spoon the squash into a serving dish and garnish with the chopped hazelnuts.

Savory Lentils with Horseradish Cream
Serves 4

Top these flavorful lentils from Rob Pounding of Salishan Lodge, Gleneden Beach, Oregon, with smoked salmon or Spiced Duck Legs (page 72) for a hearty meal.

>   2 *bacon slices, diced*
>   1 *onion, diced*
>   1 *celery stalk, diced*
>   1 *carrot, diced*
>   1 *apple, peeled and diced*
>   2 *cups apple juice*
>   1 *cup water*
>   1 *cup lentils, rinsed in cold water*
>   2 *teaspoons minced fresh oregano*

Horseradish Cream
>   1 *cup whipping cream*
>   1 *tablespoon prepared horseradish*
>   1 *tablespoon chopped chives*

In a skillet over medium heat, sauté the bacon, onion, celery, and carrot for about 15 minutes, or until tender. Add the apple and sauté for another minute, then add the apple juice and water. Stir in the lentils and cook, covered, for about 1 hour, or until tender, stirring occasionally to prevent sticking. Stir in the oregano.

Whip the cream until it forms soft peaks. Fold in the horseradish and chopped chives.

To serve, top the lentils with smoked salmon or duck and garnish with a dollop of Horseradish cream.

Warm Tea-Smoked Chicken Salad with Hazelnut Dressing

Serves 2 as a main course

Delicately flavored slices of tea-smoked chicken, toasted hazelnuts, celery, and red grapes are topped with a rich, nutty-flavored dressing. The tea-smoked chicken should be prepared at least ½ hour in advance.

Dry Marinade

½ teaspoon paprika
½ teaspoon ground coriander
¼ teaspoon salt
¼ teaspoon freshly ground black pepper
1 teaspoon sugar

2 8-ounce chicken breasts, bone in
3 tablespoons oolong tea leaves (or other smoky-flavored tea)

2 cups red leaf lettuce leaves, washed and torn into bite-size pieces
2 cups butter lettuce leaves, washed and torn into bite-size pieces
1 cup seedless red grapes
2 celery stalks, thinly sliced
4 radishes, thinly sliced

Dressing

¾ cup balsamic vinegar
¼ teaspoon salt
¼ cup chopped toasted hazelnuts (page 82)

2 tablespoons hazelnut or walnut oil

Preheat the oven to 400° F.

Combine the paprika, coriander, salt, pepper, and sugar in a mixing bowl. Remove and discard the skin from the chicken breasts and rub the meat with the dry marinade. Fill a roasting pan with 2 inches of hot water and add the tea leaves. Place the chicken on a wire cake rack or broiler rack

A hazelnut oil–based dressing subtlely enhances the flavor of tea-smoked chicken.

and set the rack over the pan. Cover the chicken with foil and bake for 20 minutes. Turn the chicken, cover, and return to the oven. Continue to bake for about 50 more minutes, or until the chicken is thoroughly cooked. Allow the chicken to cool slightly, then tear into bite-size pieces.

Arrange the greens on 2 large plates. Top each bed of greens with the grapes, celery, radishes, and shredded chicken.

Combine the oil, vinegar, and salt in a saucepan and bring to a boil. Pour the hot dressing over the salads and top with the hazelnuts.

Recommended wines: *Pinot Gris, Chardonnay, dry Riesling*

Blackberry, Tarragon, and Hazelnut Vinaigrette

Serves 4

This dressing is delicious served over a salad of fresh greens topped with Walla Walla Sweet onions, crumbled blue cheese, and toasted hazelnuts. To make blackberry vinegar, place 1 cup ripe blackberries in a glass bottle. Pour 3 cups cider vinegar over the berries and let steep at least 24 hours before using.

6 tablespoons blackberry vinegar
2 tablespoons minced fresh tarragon leaves
2 teaspoons prepared stone-ground mustard
1 tablespoon hazelnut oil
2 teaspoons sesame oil
1 garlic clove, minced
Salt and freshly ground black pepper to taste

Combine all of the ingredients in a nonreactive jar or mixing bowl and mix well. Store, covered, up to 1 week in the refrigerator.

Chicken and Noodle Casserole
Serves 4

Lori's grandma taught cooking at the high school in Bremerton, Washington. She loved to cook and always sought out the best-quality ingredients. Of all the meals she prepared, Lori's favorite was chicken and noodles. The night before, she rolled out thin golden sheets of homemade egg pasta, which she dusted with flour and covered with a dish towel to dry. The next morning, she sliced the pasta into ¼-inch ribbons, scattering the noodles over the counter to dry further. She baked them in a casserole dish with a plump, locally raised chicken and its juices, all topped with grated cheddar cheese.

If you prefer, you can substitute 6 ounces dried or fresh fettuccine noodles for the homemade pasta in this recipe. If you make your own noodles, plan to make them at least 4 hours ahead.

Noodles
- *1 cup unbleached all-purpose flour*
- *1 large egg*
- *½ teaspoon salt*
- *1½ to 2 tablespoons heavy cream*

Chicken
- *2 garlic cloves, minced*
- *2 carrots, diced*
- *1 medium onion, diced*
- *1 3½-pound roasting chicken, cut into serving pieces*
- *2 teaspoons salt*
- *½ teaspoon freshly grated black pepper*

- *½ cup grated sharp cheddar cheese*

Make the noodles: In the bowl of a food processor fitted with a metal blade, combine the flour, egg, salt, and 1½ tablespoons cream. Process until the mixture forms a ball, adding more cream if necessary. Transfer the dough to a floured surface and knead lightly. Shape into a flat round; cover with a towel and let the dough rest 15 minutes to relax the gluten.

Roll the dough out on a floured surface to ⅛-inch thickness (this will form a rectangle about 12 × 16 inches). Dust with flour, cover with a dish towel, and let dry for at least 3 hours or overnight. Slice the pasta into ¼-inch-wide × 3-inch-long noodles. Cover with the dish towel and let dry at least 1 hour or overnight:

Prepare the chicken: Place the garlic, carrots, and onion in the bottom of a large saucepan. Lay the chicken pieces over the vegetables; sprinkle with the salt and pepper and cover with 4 cups cold water. Bring the water to a boil over high heat. As soon as the water begins to boil, turn off the heat and cover the pan. Let the chicken sit, covered, on the burner for 30 minutes, or until cooked through.

Remove the chicken from the broth, reserving 1¼ cups of broth and the cooked vegetables. Once the chicken is cool enough to handle, remove the meat from the bones and set aside.

Meanwhile, bring 4 cups of water to a boil over high heat. Stir in the noodles and cook just until tender, about 3 minutes. Pour the noodles into a colander and rinse under cold running water. Drain.

Preheat the oven to 375° F. Grease the bottom of a 1-quart casserole dish. Scatter one-third of the noodles in the dish. Top with one-third of the chicken. Repeat with the remaining noodles and chicken until they are used up. Pour the reserved broth and vegetables over all. Cover the casserole and bake for about 30 minutes, or until hot. Uncover, top with the cheddar cheese, and place under the broiler until the cheese is hot and bubbly, about 3 minutes.

Recommended wines: *Pinot Gris, Sauvignon Blanc, Semillon*

Chicken in Pinot Noir with Wild Mushrooms and Bacon
Serves 4

This is a northwestern rendition of the classic French dish coq au vin. It's simple to prepare and all you need to serve with it is a simple salad, a loaf of bread (to soak up the tasty sauce), and a bottle of Pinot Noir.

  2 tablespoons olive oil
  1 4-pound roasting chicken, cut into serving pieces
     Flour, for dusting the chicken
  2 tablespoons brandy
  2 cups Pinot Noir
  4 bacon slices, cut into ½-inch pieces
 10 small onions, or 2 large onions, quartered
  4 ounces fresh porcini, cèpes, chanterelles, or other wild mushrooms, diced

In a large, heavy-bottomed skillet, heat the olive oil over medium heat. Dust the chicken with the flour and sauté it in the oil until golden, about 3 to 5 minutes on each side. You may need to cook the chicken in batches.

Drain the cooking liquid from the pan. Pour the brandy into a warmed soup ladle and ignite with a match or cigarette lighter. (Stand back, but don't panic, the flames may look scary, but they are really harmless.) Pour the ignited brandy over the chicken and let the flames die out.

Pour the wine over the chicken and bring to a boil. Then reduce the heat, cover, and simmer until the chicken is tender, about 30 minutes.

In the meantime, in a skillet, sauté the bacon over medium heat for about 3 minutes. Add the onions and mushrooms and cook over low heat until tender.

When the chicken is cooked, drain the cooking liquid into the mushroom-bacon mixture and simmer rapidly, stirring often, until the liquid has reduced to a syruplike consistency, about 12 to 15 minutes. Add the chicken pieces to the sauce and serve immediately.

Recommended wine: *Pinot Noir*

Dried Cherry Marinated Chicken
Serves 4

Dried Chuckar cherries from eastern Washington are a favorite with northwestern locals. Here their rich flavor is combined with a northwestern Pinot Noir wine and used as a marinade for grilled chicken. Chefs Caprial and John Pence of Portland's Westmoreland Bistro serve this chicken over mixed greens accompanied by grilled vegetables like summer squash, endive, and tomatoes. Allow at least 4 hours to marinate the chicken.

Marinade
  ½ cup dried cherries
  ¼ cup Pinot Noir or other dry red wine
  ¼ cup olive oil
  2 shallots, finely diced
  2 garlic cloves, minced

  4 medium chicken breasts

In a large saucepan, combine the cherries, wine, olive oil, shallots, and garlic. Bring the mixture to a boil, then remove the pan from the heat and let the mixture cool to room temperature.

Place the chicken breasts in a flat, nonreactive pan. Pour the marinade over the chicken. Cover and chill 4 hours, or overnight, turning once or twice.

Preheat the barbecue or grill. Grill the chicken over the hot coals, basting with the marinade and turning occasionally, for about 15 minutes, or until cooked through.

Recommended wine: *Pinot Noir*

Country Salmon Pie
Serves 8 to 10

This savory pie from the Shelburne Inn is delicious for brunch warm from the oven.

Parmesan Crust
2½ cups all-purpose flour
¾ cup finely grated Parmesan cheese
10 tablespoons unsalted butter, chilled
3 tablespoons cold water

Smoked Salmon Filling
3 tablespoons unsalted butter
1 garlic clove, minced
1 large onion, diced
2¼ cups sour cream
5 large eggs
1½ cups grated Gruyère or Swiss cheese
1 tablespoon chopped fresh dill
¼ teaspoon salt
2 cups flaked smoked salmon

Preheat the oven to 375° F. In a mixing bowl, combine the flour and the parmesan. Cut in the butter until it is the size of small peas. Sprinkle the water over the flour, mixing until a dough begins to form. Press the dough into the bottom and up the sides of a 10-inch springform pan and chill for 15 minutes. Press a piece of foil over the crust to hold it in place while it bakes. Bake the crust for 10 minutes, then remove the foil and bake 3 minutes longer. Cool.

Heat the butter in a skillet over medium heat. Add the garlic and onion and sauté until softened. In a large mixing bowl, beat the sour cream and eggs together until well blended. Stir in the garlic and onion, 1 cup of the cheese, the dill, and the salt, and mix well; stir in the salmon. Pour the mixture into the prebaked crust, and top with the remaining ½ cup of grated cheese.

Bake the pie for about 1 hour, or until golden brown and firm. Let the pie cool for 15 minutes, then divide into wedges.

Spiced Duck Legs
Serves 4

In this recipe from Michael Wild of the Baywolf Restaurant in Oakland, California, duck legs are rubbed with a spicy dry marinade and dry-cured in the refrigerator for 3 to 5 days, a process that infuses them with flavor. Serve them warm on a bed of Savory Lentils with Horseradish Cream (page 65) with sautéed escarole and mushrooms cooked with garlic and onions.

> 2   *teaspoons kosher salt*
> 1   *tablespoon herbes de Provence, or a mixture of thyme, bay leaf, and marjoram*
> ½   *teaspoon hot red pepper flakes*
> 1   *teaspoon juniper berries*
> 1   *teaspoon black peppercorns*
> 1   *teaspoon allspice berries*
> 2   *whole cloves*
> 1   *½-inch cinnamon stick*
> ½   *teaspoon mustard seed*
> 1   *head of garlic, divided, peeled*
>
> 4   *duck legs, rinsed and trimmed*

Combine the salt, herbes de Provence, red pepper flakes, juniper berries, black peppercorns, allspice, cloves, cinnamon, and mustard seed in a blender or food processor and pulverize until reduced to a coarse grind. Add the garlic cloves and process until it is reduced to fine pieces.

Coat each duck leg thoroughly with the spice mixture. Layer the duck in a nonreactive pan, cover loosely with plastic wrap, and dry-cure in the refrigerator for 3 to 5 days.

To cook, preheat the oven to 375° F. Place the duck legs on a baking sheet and bake for about 45 minutes, or until crisp and golden on the outside.

Recommended wines: *Zinfandel, Pinot Noir*

Duck Breast with Chanterelle Mushroom Sauce
Serves 2

Golden apricot-scented chanterelle mushrooms (*Cantharellus cibarius*) begin to pop up in the Northwest's forests as soon as the first fall rain comes. Their sweet woodsy flavor is a delicious complement to the earthy flavor of succulent duck breast in this recipe from Table for Two in Portland, Oregon.

> 3   *tablespoons unsalted butter*
> 2   *skinless boneless duck breast halves*
> 2   *garlic cloves, minced*
> 1   *cup sliced fresh chanterelle mushrooms*
> ¼   *cup tawny port*
>   *Freshly ground black pepper*

Preheat the oven to 200° F.

Heat 2 tablespoons of the butter in a skillet over medium-high heat until it begins to bubble. Add the duck breasts and sauté for about 3 minutes on each side (the center of the breast should remain slightly pink). Keep the duck warm in the oven.

In the same skillet, heat the remaining tablespoon of butter over low heat. Stir in the garlic and mushrooms and sauté about 2 minutes, or until soft. Add the port and continue cooking for 1 more minute. Season to taste with the pepper.

Slice each duck breast into 4 pieces and fan out on individual serving plates. Top with the sauce and serve immediately.

Recommended wines: *Full-bodied Chardonnay, Pinot Noir*

Fraser Valley Pheasant with Okanagan Peach Sauce
Serves 2

Gary Faessler lives in a restored 1950s farm-house in B.C.'s Fraser Valley. One summer afternoon his cat delivered a wild pheasant to his doorstep, which prompted Gary to create this delicious recipe. He combines the Okanagan Valley's renowned peaches with Ehrenfelser wine, a rich, fruity wine packed with flavors of fresh peaches and apricots that are also grown in the Okanagan Valley, to make a fragrant sauce. If you can't locate Ehrenfelser, substitute a fruity Riesling.

    1   2½ to 3 pound free range or wild
         pheasant
4 to 5   tablespoons unsalted butter
    ½   cup Ehrenfelser or Riesling wine
    1   large shallot, minced
    1   teaspoon brown sugar
    ⅛   teaspoon ground cumin
    ⅛   teaspoon cinnamon
    2   peaches, peeled and diced into 1-inch
         cubes
         Chopped fresh tarragon for garnish

Preheat the over to 200° F. Debone and skin the pheasant, separating the breast and thigh portions from the carcass. Melt 1 tablespoon of the butter in a large skillet over medium heat. Sauté the breast and thigh portions on each side until they are light brown and cooked to medium rare, about 4 minutes per side. Transfer the pheasant to an ovenproof dish and keep warm in the oven while preparing the sauce.

Place the skillet containing the pan juices over medium-high heat; add the wine and stir briskly to deglaze the pan. Stir in the shallot, sugar, and spices and cook until the sauce is reduced to one third its original volume. Add the peaches and stir for a minute or so, until just heated through.

Remove the skillet from the heat and stir in the remaining butter, one small piece at a time. Place a pheasant breast and thigh on each of 2 warm plates, and spoon some of the sauce over each serving. Sprinkle with chopped tarragon.

Recommended wine: *Ehrenfelser*

Rabbit Sausage-Wild Mushroom Sauce for Pasta or Polenta
Serves 4

Fred Carlo is a sausage maker in Portland, Oregon. After working long hours at his two retail stores, he often relaxes at home by cooking pasta or polenta topped with a spicy sauce like this one.

    6   rabbit sausages or hot Italian sausages
    2   tablespoons olive oil
    8   ounces fresh chanterelle, cèpe, or porcini
         mushrooms, chopped
    1   onion, diced
    2   garlic cloves, minced
    1   cup dry white wine
         Juice of 1 lemon
         Salt and freshly ground black pepper
         Hot red pepper flakes

Slit the sausage skins and remove the meat from the casings, breaking it up with your fingers. Heat the olive oil in a heavy skillet, add the sausage meat, and sauté over medium heat, stirring often, until it is thoroughly cooked. With a slotted spoon, transfer the sausage to a bowl and set aside.

In the same pan, sauté the mushrooms, onion, and garlic until tender, about 12 minutes. Stir in the wine, then add the cooked sausage and simmer the sauce over low heat for 30 to 35 minutes, stirring often.

Stir in the lemon juice and season to taste with salt, black pepper, and red pepper flakes. Ladle the sauce over pasta or polenta.

Recommended wines: *Cabernet Sauvignon, Merlot, Zinfandel*

Northwestern Berries

THE PACIFIC NORTHWEST—with its mild climate and rich soil—is blessed with an abundance of berries, both wild and cultivated. Just about everyone who was raised here has special memories of berry picking. Fresh from the bush or vine, berries are one of nature's most delicious foods.

Edible berries were, and still are, highly regarded by Native Americans in the Northwest. Many of the berries collected—salal, blackberries, black raspberries, elderberries, and Oregon grape (which was often mixed with other berries to temper its sour flavor), were eaten fresh, mashed or boiled, or dried for later use. Mashed berries were often sun-dried or cooked in bentwood cedar boxes with red-hot rocks. The thickened "jam" was then poured into cedar frames lined with skunk cabbage leaves, where it was dried over a slow fire. The resulting fruit leather was rolled and stored for later use.

According to ethnobotanist Nancy J. Turner of British Columbia, the Nootka Indians of British Columbia prepared a special type of roasted clam and thimbleberry cake. This was made by laying out skewers of roasted clams on a board and covering them with a layer of fresh thimbleberries. The layering was repeated and a heavy plank was placed on top to flatten the cakes, after which the cakes were sun-dried.

The Kwakiutl Indians often picked thimbleberries green with their stems attached, sprinkled them with water, and left them to ripen in cedar bark bags. Black caps, a variety of wild raspberry easily identified by the blue-gray bloom on the rosy stalks and fruit, were sun-dried like raisins, a technique that also works well with wild trailing blackberries and cranberries.

Top and right: **Granger Berry Farm in Washington** grows more than twenty-five varieties of berries. *Opposite:* **A medley of fresh local berries.**

Lamb Stew with Seasonal Vegetables
Serves 6 to 8

This colorful stew, from Chef Bruno Marti, is the very best kind of one-dish meal.

¼ cup olive oil
3 pounds lamb shoulder, cubed
2 garlic cloves, minced
¾ cup sliced fennel
1 onion, diced
¼ cup tomato paste
3¾ cups dry red wine
12 fresh sage leaves, minced
2 medium potatoes, peeled and cubed
1 small (8-ounce) butternut squash, peeled, seeded, and cubed
18 pearl onions, peeled
18 mushrooms, halved
2 carrots, chopped
Salt and freshly ground black pepper to taste
6 to 8 whole sage leaves, for garnish

Preheat the oven to 375° F.

Melt 2 tablespoons of the olive oil in a heavy-bottomed skillet over medium-high heat. Sauté the lamb, turning often, for about 5 minutes, or until the lamb is browned on all sides.

Add the garlic, fennel, and onion and sauté 2 minutes longer. Stir in the tomato paste, red wine, and sage, scraping up any brown bits on the bottom of the pan, and turn the mixture into a large ovenproof casserole dish. Top with the potatoes. Cover and bake for about 1½ hours, or until the lamb is tender.

About ½ hour before the lamb has finished cooking, sauté the squash, onions, mushrooms, and carrots in the remaining 2 tablespoons olive oil over medium heat for about 5 minutes. Add ½ cup water and simmer until tender, about 15 minutes.

Season the vegetables lightly with salt and pepper.

Remove the lamb casserole from the oven and spoon the sautéed vegetables over the top. Garnish with whole sage leaves, if desired.

Recommended wines: *Merlot, Cabernet Sauvignon*

Warm Slivered Lamb with Creamy Garlic Dressing
Serves 2 as a main course

Tender, earthy-flavored spring lamb is plentiful in the Northwest. Here it's combined in a hearty salad with spinach, new potatoes, and broccoli, all topped with a robust garlicky dressing.

Marinade
2 garlic cloves, minced
¼ cup dry red wine
1 tablespoon olive oil
8 to 12 ounces lamb from the leg, loin, or shoulder (4 to 6 ounces per serving)

4 small red potatoes, cut into ½-inch slices
2 cups broccoli florets
2 bunches of spinach, rinsed, stemmed, and dried

Dressing
1 cup crème fraîche
2 teaspoons prepared stone-ground or Dijon-style mustard
3 garlic cloves, minced
2 teaspoons capers, drained
2 tablespoons cider vinegar
Salt, to taste

1 to 2 teaspoons olive oil
½ red onion, thinly sliced

One to three hours in advance, prepare the marinade by mixing the garlic, wine, and olive oil in a nonreactive bowl. Add the lamb and marinate until cooking time.

Place the potatoes in a saucepan, cover with cold water, and bring to a boil. Reduce the heat and simmer until just tender, about 10 minutes. Drain and set the potatoes aside. Place the broccoli in the same pan, cover with cold water, bring to a boil, and cook for about 5 minutes, or until just tender. Drain and rinse immediately in cold water (this preserves the bright green color).

Tear the spinach into bite-size pieces and arrange on 2 large serving plates. Arrange the potatoes and broccoli alternately around the edges of each plate. Drain the marinade from the lamb and slice the lamb into long, 1/4-inch-thick slivers.

To make the dressing, combine the crème fraîche, mustard, garlic, capers, vinegar, and salt in a saucepan and bring to a boil. Continue to boil for approximately 5 minutes, or until slightly thickened. Keep warm.

Meanwhile, heat 1 to 2 teaspoons of olive oil in a skillet over medium heat. Sauté the lamb about 8 to 10 minutes, until it is cooked but still slightly pink in the center. Spoon the hot lamb over the greens and pour the hot dressing over the top. Distribute the sliced red onion over the salad.

Recommended wines: *Cabernet Sauvignon, Merlot, Zinfandel*

Grilled Fillet of Beef on Mixed Greens with Oregon Blue Cheese Dressing
Serves 4

Gary Faessler purchases organic beef from the Rodear Cattle Ranch, located near Williams Lake in British Columbia's Cariboo country. "This is the first government-certified and -inspected organic meat processing plant in western Canada," says Faessler. "This small family-owned opera-

tion is run by David Fernie and his parents, Allan and Carole, who have a back-to-nature method of raising cattle." The cattle feed on the unsprayed grasslands of the Cariboo, and are finished on certified organic grains.

1   *pound fillet of beef tenderloin*
1   *tablespoon hazelnut or olive oil*

4   *ounces Oregon blue cheese, crumbled*
3/4   *cup plain yogurt*
1/3   *cup sour cream*
1   *tablespoon lime juice*
     Freshly ground black pepper to taste
8   *cups mixed greens, such as romaine, red leaf lettuce, radicchio, mustard greens, arugula, or endive*
1   *large tomato, finely diced*

Rub the beef lightly on both sides with the oil. Grill over high heat, approximately 5 to 7 minutes per side, until the meat is cooked rare.

Meanwhile, make the dressing by combining the blue cheese, yogurt, sour cream, lime juice, and pepper.

Divide the salad greens among 4 large plates. Top with the diced tomato. Slice the beef across the grain into 1-inch-thick pieces and arrange a few slices on each serving. Spoon the dressing over the salads and serve.

Recommended wine: *Cabernet Sauvignon*

Cranberry Pot Roast
Serves 6 to 8

The Shelburne Inn is located on the Longview Peninsula in southwestern Washington, where cranberry bogs are a common site. In this recipe, Laurie Anderson combines local cranberries with Oregon Pinot Noir and spices to make a tart sauce, which she serves with fork-tender pot roast and Baked Butternut Squash with Hazelnuts (page 65).

   3 *tablespoons unbleached all-purpose flour*
   1 *teaspoon salt*
  ¼ *teaspoon black pepper*
   1 *3- to 4-pound rump roast or brisket*
   3 *tablespoons vegetable oil*
   1 *onion, thinly sliced*
   1 *garlic clove, minced*
   4 *whole cloves*
   1 *cinnamon stick*
  ¾ *cup beef broth*

Cranberry Sauce
   1 *cup sugar*
   1 *cup Pinot Noir or other dry red wine*
   1 *12-ounce package cranberries, fresh or frozen*
   1 *tablespoon white vinegar*
   1 *orange, unpeeled, very thinly sliced*
   6 *whole cloves*
   1 *cinnamon stick*

Combine the flour, salt, and pepper and rub into the pot roast on each side, using all of the mixture. Heat 1 tablespoon of the vegetable oil over medium heat in a large, heavy-bottomed skillet. Sauté the onion and garlic until translucent, about 5 minutes, then transfer to a small bowl and set aside. Increase the heat under the skillet to medium-high, add the remaining oil, and brown the meat on all sides. Remove the pan from the heat. Add the cloves, cinnamon, sautéed onion and garlic, and beef broth to the pot roast.

Cover tightly and simmer over low heat about 2½ hours, or until the meat is very tender. If the pan becomes dry, add more beef broth or water as necessary, keeping about 1½ inches of liquid in the bottom of the pan at all times.

While the meat is cooking, prepare the cranberry sauce. In a saucepan, combine the sugar and wine and bring the mixture to a boil. Add the cranberries, vinegar, orange slices, cloves, and cinnamon and simmer the mixture gently for 15 to 20 minutes.

Once the meat has finished cooking, use a large spoon to skim the fat from the broth. Add the cranberry sauce to the pot roast. Cover and cook 10 to 15 minutes longer, or until the sauce is heated through. Remove and discard the cinnamon stick and orange slices. Transfer the meat to a serving platter and slice thinly. Ladle some of the sauce over the pot roast and pass the extra sauce separately.

Recommended wine: *Pinot Noir*

Dried cranberries add tangy flavor to this savory pot roast.

Italian Country Bread
Makes 2 round loaves

Many Italians immigrated to the Pacific Northwest during the late 1800s and early 1900s. A number of them raised "truck gardens" and hauled their fresh produce from the farms to the city markets to sell. This recipe comes from a friend whose Italian nana was an excellent baker; dusted with flour, her round, free-form loaves have a real country look and flavor.

> 2 teaspoons active dry yeast
> 1/4 cup warm water
> 2 cups Sourdough Starter (page 160)
> 1 tablespoon sugar
>   Approximately 5 cups unbleached all-purpose flour
> 2 tablespoons olive oil
> 2 teaspoons salt
>   Cornmeal, to sprinkle on the baking sheets

In a large mixing bowl, dissolve the yeast in the warm water for about 5 minutes. Stir in the sourdough starter, mixing well. Add the sugar, 1 cup of flour, olive oil, and salt. Stir in the remaining flour 1 cup at a time, until the dough is stiff and can be kneaded.

Turn the dough onto a floured surface and knead approximately 10 minutes, incorporating more flour as needed. Place the dough in a large, well-oiled mixing bowl and cover with plastic wrap. Let rise in a warm place until the dough has doubled in bulk, about 1 1/2 hours.

Preheat the oven to 350° F.

Once the dough has risen, punch down and turn out onto a floured surface. Divide the dough into 2 pieces and shape each into a round loaf. Set loaves on a well-oiled baking sheet dusted with cornmeal. Rub the tops of the loaves with flour. Using a sharp knife or a razor blade, make narrow slits across the top surface of the bread about 1/2 inch apart. Allow the bread to rise about 1/2 hour, or until the bread springs back immediately when you press your finger lightly into the dough.

Bake the bread approximately 30 minutes, or until the tops and bottoms of the loaves are golden and the bread sounds hollow when tapped with a finger.

Highland Toasted Oat Bread
Makes 2 round loaves

During the mid-1800s a group of immigrants from the highlands of Scotland arrived in the Northwest to work as shepherds. As sheep herders on the open range, their job was to keep the herds together, making sure the sheep were properly fed. Taking care of a large flock left little time for cooking and eating. The shepherd's dinner, often prepared by lantern light, generally consisted of fried mutton, beans, potatoes, hardtack or bread, dried prunes, and coffee.

Toasted oats give this golden bread a chewy texture and nutty flavor.

> 2 cups rolled oats
> 2 tablespoons 2-ounce (1/2 packet) active dry yeast, or 1 cake fresh yeast, crumbled
> 1/4 cup plus 2 tablespoons firmly packed light brown sugar
> 2 cups warm water
> 2 large eggs, lightly beaten
> 2 tablespoons vegetable oil
> 2 cups whole wheat flour
> 1 tablespoon salt
> 3 to 4 cups unbleached all-purpose flour (approximately)
>   Cornmeal, to sprinkle on the baking sheets

Preheat the oven to 350° F. Spread the oats on a cookie sheet and toast in the oven for about 15 minutes, stirring occasionally, until golden brown. Set aside to cool.

Chuck Wagon Cooking

WHAT DID COWBOYS *really eat? Fried Rocky Mountain oysters (bull's testicles), for one. Other traditional cowboy dishes included "son-of-a-bitch" stew, made with whatever meat was handy (including heart, liver, sweetbreads, brains, and marrow gut), groat clusters (pancakes), cow sap (milk), cackleberries (eggs), sow belly (bacon), pecos strawberries (pinto beans), corn bread, and sourdough biscuits.*

The chuck wagon, a rolling kitchen built on a rudimentary wagon from which the cook prepared all of the meals, was an integral part of the cowboy's life. During roundup, the cowboys fanned out from the moving chuck wagon, circling back to it each evening with their cattle. Before turning in at night, the cook pointed the chuck wagon toward the north star, which acted as a compass for the trail boss setting out in the morning.

Before the invention of the chuck wagon in 1866 by Charles Goodnight, cowboys carried and cooked their own meals. Goodnight designed his first chuck wagon around a surplus army wagon, which he fitted with a large water barrel, a toolbox, a canopy frame to provide protection against sun and rain, and, most important, a chuck box (chuck was cowboy slang for food), which, fitted with drawers and cubbyholes, held the cook's provisions. A boot beneath the chuck box held the cook's utensils and a calfskin hammock suspended under the wagon carried a collection of "prairie coal"—usually dried cow or buffalo manure, which was kindled with bacon rind.

Typical provisions on the chuck wagon included flour, sugar, dried fruit, pinto beans, salt, vinegar, a sourdough keg, castor oil, molasses, whiskey (for medicinal purposes), and coffee to make powerfully strong black "cowboy coffee."

Beef was a rarity in the cowboy's diet: It wasn't economical to kill cattle on the trail. If time allowed for hunting, fresh meat might be provided by a rabbit or deer, but that was uncommon. Fresh vegetables and fruits, eggs, milk, and desserts were also generally absent from the chuckwagon menu.

In a large mixing bowl, combine the yeast and 2 tablespoons of the brown sugar. Pour in the water and let the mixture sit about 5 minutes, or until the yeast starts to bubble. Stir in the eggs, the remaining brown sugar, oil, whole wheat flour, and salt, mixing well. Stir in the toasted oats, then add the unbleached flour 1 cup at a time, until a stiff dough is formed.

Turn the dough onto a floured surface and knead for 10 minutes, adding more flour as necessary to prevent sticking. Place the dough in a well-oiled bowl and cover with plastic wrap. Set the dough in a warm place for about 1 hour, or until doubled in bulk.

Turn out onto a floured surface and divide the dough into 2 pieces. Shape into round loaves. Set on a well-oiled baking sheet sprinkled with cornmeal. With a sharp knife or a razor blade, cut crisscross slits (2 in each direction) across the top of each loaf. Let the bread rise about 1/2 hour, or until doubled in bulk.

Bake in a 350° F. oven for about 30 to 40 minutes, or until the loaves are golden brown and sound hollow when tapped.

Above: **A** variety of **N**orthwest breads and cheeses. *Opposite:* **H**azelnut-**P**ort **B**aguettes.

Toasted Hazelnut-Port Baguettes
Makes 2 loaves

Lee Gray combines two sophisticated flavorings in these elegant baguettes.

1½ tablespoons active dry yeast
½ cup warm water
½ cup port or other red wine
½ cup chopped roasted hazelnuts
1 teaspoon salt
2 to 2½ cups unbleached all-purpose flour
Cornmeal, to sprinkle on the baking sheets

Combine the yeast and warm water in a large mixing bowl and let sit about 5 minutes, or until the yeast has dissolved. Stir in the port, hazelnuts, salt, and 2 cups of the flour, mixing thoroughly.

Gradually add more flour, mixing thoroughly after each addition, until the mixture pulls away from the sides of the mixing bowl.

Turn the dough onto a floured surface and knead, adding more flour as necessary to prevent the dough from sticking. Continue to knead for about 5 minutes, then turn the dough into a well-oiled mixing bowl. Cover with plastic wrap or a damp cloth and set in a warm place to rise until doubled in bulk, about 2 to 3 hours.

Turn the dough onto a floured surface and pat down flat. Cut the dough into 2 equal portions and roll each into a ball. Let the dough sit for 10 minutes to relax the gluten, then, using the palms of your hands, roll each ball on the floured surface to create a long baguette.

Transfer the baguettes to well-oiled baking sheets that have been dusted with cornmeal. Set in a warm place and let rise until a finger pressed into the dough leaves no impression, about 45 minutes to 1 hour.

Preheat the oven to 400° F.

Slice the baguettes lengthwise with a razor blade or sharp knife to make a ¼-inch-deep slit in the top of each loaf. Mist the baguettes lightly with water and place in the hot oven. Continue to mist the bread lightly every 5 minutes or so as they bake. Bake the baguettes about 25 to 30 minutes, or until they are golden brown and sound hollow when tapped with your finger. Transfer to a cooling rack. Serve warm or at room temperature.

Toasting Nuts

Preheat the oven to 350° F.

Distribute nuts evenly over a cookie sheet in a single layer. Toast in the oven, stirring occasionally, until the nuts are brown and fragrant, about 10 to 15 minutes. Cool. **N**ote: To remove the papery skins from hazelnuts, gather the nuts in a dish towel and rub briskly in the towel.

Apple-Raisin Quick Bread
Makes one 8 × 5-inch loaf

Served with sharp cheddar cheese, this moist bread is delicious for breakfast or an afternoon snack. Tart, crisp apples like Gravensteins or Granny Smiths work best in this recipe.

> 2 cups unbleached all-purpose flour
> ½ teaspoon baking soda
> 1 teaspoon baking powder
> 1 teaspoon salt
> ½ cup (1 stick) unsalted butter, melted
> ⅔ cup sugar
> 3 large eggs, slightly beaten
> ¼ cup applesauce
> ¼ cup plain nonfat yogurt
> 1 cup peeled finely diced apples
> ½ cup grated sharp cheddar cheese
> ¼ cup chopped walnuts
> ½ cup raisins
>
> Juice of 1 lemon
> 1 tablespoon sugar
> 1 teaspoon cinnamon

Preheat the oven to 350° F. Grease and flour an 8 × 5-inch loaf pan.

Sift together the flour, baking soda, baking powder, and salt. In a mixing bowl, combine the melted butter with the ⅔ cup sugar; stir until thoroughly blended. Stir in the eggs, applesauce, yogurt, diced apples, cheese, nuts, and raisins. Stir in the flour mixture, mixing well.

Turn the batter into the prepared loaf pan. Bake for about 1 hour, or until a toothpick inserted in the center comes out clean. Remove the bread from the oven and sprinkle with the lemon juice, the 1 tablespoon sugar, and the cinnamon. Return to the oven and bake 5 to 8 minutes longer. Let set in the pan for 5 minutes. Transfer to a cooling rack and cool before slicing.

Peach Conserve
Makes about 2 pints

U-pick peach orchards dot the Northwest countryside. For just a few dollars you can strap yourself into a peach-picking harness and load up with the juiciest peaches imaginable.

> 4 cups coarsely chopped peaches
> ½ cup coarsely chopped Italian plums
> ⅓ cup seedless raisins
> 1 medium orange, seeded and ground in a
>   food process or food grinder
> 1 cup light corn syrup

Place the peaches, plums, and raisins in a large, heavy-bottomed saucepan. Stir in the orange, ½ cup water, and the corn syrup. Bring the mixture to a boil; reduce the heat and simmer until dark and thick, about 1 hour. Store in the refrigerator up to 1 week, or seal in hot sterilized jars and process in a hot water bath to store indefinitely.

Pear-Cranberry Chutney
Makes 6 pints

This tart, colorful chutney makes a wonderful condiment for turkey, chicken, or pork. It will keep up to 2 weeks stored in the refrigerator or it can be canned.

> 2 12-ounce packages fresh cranberries
> 5 large pears, peeled and chopped
> 3 garlic cloves, minced
> 2 tablespoons grated fresh gingerroot
> 1 teaspoon red pepper flakes
> 2 onions, diced
> 3½ cups sugar
> ¼ cup dark molasses
> 3 cups cider vinegar
> 1 cup raisins

Combine all the ingredients in a large, heavy-bottomed saucepan. Bring to a boil over medium-high heat, stirring often. Reduce the heat to a simmer and cook about 1½ hours, stirring occasionally, until the mixture is thickened. To test, set a small plate in the freezer until very cold. Drop a teaspoonful of the chutney on the cold plate; the chutney should firm up on the plate. If not, continue cooking. Retest every few minutes.

Ladle the hot chutney into 6 sterilized pint-capacity jars and refrigerate process in a water bath to store indefinitely.

Peach Chutney
Makes 3 to 4 pints

2½ pounds fresh peaches or nectarines, peeled, pitted, and coarsely chopped
1 tart green apple, peeled, cored, and coarsely chopped
¼ cup orange juice
¼ cup fresh lime or lemon juice
2 cups brown sugar
1 cup raisins
¼ cup cider vinegar
½ teaspoon ground cinnamon
1 tablespoon freshly grated gingerroot

Place peaches, apples, orange and lime juices, brown sugar, raisins, and vinegar in a large nonreactive saucepan. Bring the mixture to a boil over medium heat, then reduce the heat and allow the mixture to simmer, stirring occasionally, for about 1½ hours, or until thickened. Remove from the heat and stir in the spices. Cool the chutney thoroughly, and refrigerate for up to 2 weeks, or ladle into sterilized jars and process in a hot water bath.

Northwest Apricot Butter
Makes about 2 pints

Jeanne gathers fresh apricots from the tree growing beside her Orcas Island garden for use in these fragrant preserves. Alexander loves to eat this for breakfast, either mixed with yogurt or as a topping for French toast or pancakes.

20 extra-ripe apricots
Sugar, as needed

Dip the apricots briefly into boiling, then immediately into cold water to facilitate peeling. Then peel and halve the apricots, discarding the pits. Mash the fruit roughly, leaving some pieces in chunks. Measure the fruit into a large, heavy-bottomed saucepan and add 2 cups sugar for each cup of apricot pulp. Bring the mixture to a boil over medium heat, stirring constantly. Reduce the heat and simmer until thick and clear, about 30 minutes, stirring frequently to prevent scorching. Ladle the hot apricot butter into sterilized jars and refrigerate for up to 2 weeks, or process in a hot water bath to store indefinitely.

Oakridge Orchard

TOP-QUALITY ORGANIC APPLES *and pears are the focus of this small family-run orchard in White Salmon, Washington, located just an hour and a half east of Portland. Everything here, including the planting of saplings, tilling of the soil, pruning, harvesting, repairing equipment, fertilizing, and marketing, is done by Bonnie and Dennis White, often with the help of their daughter Nancy. "Small is beautiful," says Dennis. "There's a certain efficiency that you can only accomplish on a small scale, and we want to keep it this way."*

Strongly committed to organic agriculture and to preserving the environment, the Whites planted their orchard bit by bit, allowing weeds like chicory to grow between the rows of fruit trees in order to attract bees. Bats swoop through the orchard in the evenings to feed on troublesome coddling moths.

Jonagold, a cross between Jonathan and Golden Delicious, is the Whites' favorite apple for fresh eating and one of the fifteen different varieties of apples and pears they cultivate. Other apple varieties include Gravenstein, an old favorite from northern Europe; Spartan, a cross between McIntosh and Newtown Pippin; and

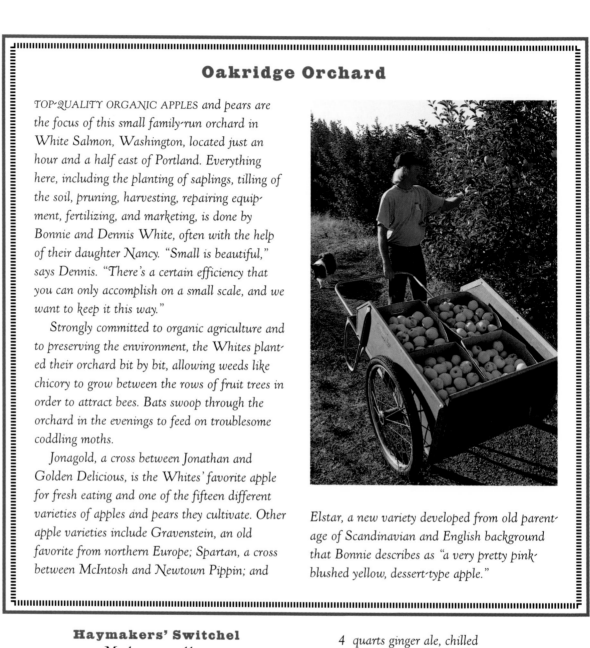

Elstar, a new variety developed from old parentage of Scandinavian and English background that Bonnie describes as "a very pretty pink-blushed yellow, dessert-type apple."

Haymakers' Switchel
Makes 1 gallon

Workers at The Herbfarm in Fall City, Washington, often enjoy this refreshing drink based on a nineteenth-century recipe after a day of labor under the hot summer sun.

¼ *cup sugar*
½ *cup water*
½ *cup finely chopped mint leaves*
½ *cup finely chopped lemon balm leaves*
¼ *cup lemon juice*
½ *cup orange juice*
4 *quarts ginger ale, chilled*
Mint leaves, for garnish

Combine the sugar and water in a large saucepan and bring to a boil, stirring often to dissolve the sugar. Add the chopped mint and lemon balm, then stir in the lemon juice and boil for 30 seconds. Turn off the heat, cover, and let stand for 1 hour.

Stir in the orange juice, then strain the mixture through a fine sieve. Just before serving, mix with chilled ginger ale. Serve garnished with fresh mint leaves.

86

Caramel Apple-Raisin Cake
Serves 12

After baking, this dense spicy cake is brushed with dark rum and topped with a chewy caramel glaze. Served with coffee or tea, it makes a great afternoon snack, or top it with ice cream for dessert.

    1   cup raisins
    4   tablespoons dark rum
    1   teaspoon vanilla extract
    ½   cup (1 stick) unsalted butter, softened
    1½   cups granulated sugar
    2   eggs
    2½   cups unbleached all-purpose flour
    2   teaspoons baking soda
    ½   teaspoon cinnamon
    ½   teaspoon nutmeg
    ½   teaspoon salt
    1   cup buttermilk
    2   large apples, cored, peeled, and roughly
         grated (2 cups loosely packed)
    ½   cup roughly chopped walnuts

Caramel Glaze

    ¼   cup heavy cream
    ¾   cup firmly packed light brown sugar

At least 1 hour in advance, place the raisins in a small bowl and sprinkle with 2 tablespoons of the rum and the vanilla. Cover and set aside until needed.

Preheat the oven to 350° F. Grease and flour a 10-inch Bundt pan.

In a mixing bowl, cream the butter until pale. Add the sugar gradually and beat until pale and fluffy. Add the eggs one at a time, beating well after each addition. Sift together the flour, baking soda, cinnamon, nutmeg, and salt. Add to the batter in 3 portions, alternating with the buttermilk.

Add the raisins and their liquid to the batter. Fold in the grated apples and the walnuts. Turn the batter into the pan and bake for about 1 hour, or until a toothpick inserted in the center comes out clean.

While the cake is baking, make the glaze. Combine the cream and brown sugar in a saucepan. Bring the mixture to a boil over high heat, reduce the heat, and continue to simmer for about 4 minutes, or until slightly thickened. Keep warm.

Turn the cake out onto a serving plate and, while it is still hot, brush the cake with the remaining 2 tablespoons rum. Let the cake sit 5 minutes to absorb the rum; spoon the hot caramel glaze over the top of the cake, letting it run down the sides.

Toasted Hazelnut Mousse
Serves 4 to 6

This soft, creamy mousse captures the essence of toasted hazelnuts. To heighten the hazelnut experience, serve with Hazelnut Shortbread (page 166).

    1¼   cups hazelnuts
    1   cup heavy cream
    6   large egg yolks, at room temperature
    ¼   cup plus 2 tablespoons sugar
    ¼   cup Frangelico or other hazelnut liqueur
    1½   tablespoons (1½ ¼-ounce packets)
         unflavored gelatin
    1½   cups heavy cream, whipped to soft peaks

Preheat the oven to 350° F.

Spread the hazelnuts on a baking sheet and bake for about 15 minutes, stirring occasionally, or until golden brown and fragrant.

Reserve 6 hazelnuts for garnish and roughly chop the remaining nuts. (It's not necessary to peel them.) Combine the chopped hazelnuts with the cream in a saucepan. Bring to a boil, then remove from the heat and let the mixture cool to room temperature. (Chill the mixture in the freezer or refrigerator if you're in a hurry.)

Strain the hazelnut mixture, reserving the liquid and discarding the nuts. In a mixing bowl, beat the egg yolks. Add the sugar gradually and continue beating until the yolks are thick and tripled in volume, about 5 minutes (they should have the texture of whipped cream).

Meanwhile, pour the liqueur into a small heatproof dish or cup. Sprinkle the gelatin over the liqueur and allow to stand for about 5 minutes, or until the gelatin has softened. Heat a double boiler filled with approximately 1 inch of water and place the cup filled with gelatin in the hot water. Heat, stirring as little as possible, until the gelatin has dissolved, about 3 minutes.

Gradually whisk the hazelnut-flavored cream into the egg yolk mixture. Stir 1 tablespoon of the hazelnut mixture into the gelatin, then pour the gelatin into the hazelnut mixture, whisking constantly. Fold in the whipped cream (reserving ¼ cup, if desired, for garnish), and pour or pipe the mousse into 4 to 6 tall dessert or wine glasses. Chill at least 3 hours, or until the mousse sets.

Garnish the hazelnut mousse with a dollop of whipped cream and the reserved hazelnuts.

Recommended wines: *Late-harvest botrytis-affected Gewürztraminer or Riesling*

Poached Pears in Cabernet Sauvignon with Crème Fraîche
Serves 6

Harvest time in British Columbia's Okanagan Valley provided the inspiration for this elegant dessert from Canadian cooking show ("Chefs About Town") host and producer Gary Faessler. "The Okanagan Valley is renowned for its tree fruits," says Faessler. "It is also British Columbia's major wine-producing area. In autumn, when the valley turns yellow and gold, pears are at their best; it's also time for the grape harvest."

Each year Gary's friend Vera Klokocka of Hillside Cellars in the Okanagan Valley makes a small amount of Cabernet

Sauvignon/Merlot, his preferred poaching liquid. Later the wine is reduced to make a flavorful sauce. "Wines with cherry, blackberry, pepper, and oak flavor notes give supreme results in this recipe," he says. Gary prefers Bosc pears in this recipe, but other varieties can be substituted. Look for pears that are ripe and fragrant but not mushy.

6 *ripe, firm pears*
Juice of 1 lemon
1 *bottle Cabernet Sauvignon*
3 *tablespoons Okanagan fireweed honey or other flavorful honey*
1 *teaspoon freshly grated nutmeg*
1 *cup crème fraîche or sour cream*

Carefully peel the pears, leaving stems and any leaves intact. Brush with lemon juice to prevent discoloration. Set aside.

In a large nonreactive saucepan, bring the wine, honey, and nutmeg to a boil. Reduce the heat and bring the liquid to a gentle simmer. Using a slotted spoon, gently slide the pears into the wine and poach for about 25 minutes, or until they are soft to the touch but still slightly firm. Lift the pears out of the wine, place them in a shallow dish, and pour 1 cup of the poaching liquid over them. Set aside.

Meanwhile, bring the poaching liquid to a rapid boil and simmer briskly until the liquid thickens slightly, about 20 minutes.

To serve, spoon 2 tablespoons of crème fraîche on each dessert plate. Place a pear in the center of the plate, then drizzle with several tablespoons of the Cabernet sauce.

Chocolate-Cherry Bars
Makes sixteen 2 x 3-inch bars

Use fresh Rainier or Bing cherries, or a combination of the two, in these chewy little confections.

Filling
- 2 cups pitted fresh cherries
- ½ cup apple juice
- 1 teaspoon vanilla extract
- 1 teaspoon lemon zest
- 1 tablespoon cornstarch
- ½ to ¾ cup granulated sugar

Cookie Dough
- 1 cup unsalted butter (2 sticks), softened to room temperature
- 1 cup firmly packed light brown sugar
- ½ cup granulated sugar
- ½ cup buttermilk
- 2 cups unbleached all-purpose flour
- 2 cups rolled oats
- ½ teaspoon cinnamon
- ¾ cup unsweetened cocoa powder

Combine the ingredients for the filling in a saucepan. Cook over medium heat for about 7 minutes, or until slightly thickened. Set aside to cool slightly.

Preheat the oven to 350° F.

Cream the butter and sugars together in a mixing bowl until pale and fluffy. Gradually add the buttermilk, then stir in the flour, oats, cinnamon, and cocoa. Pat half of the dough into the bottom of a 9 × 12-inch greased baking pan. Spread the filling over the dough. Crumble the remaining dough over the top.

Bake about 40 minutes, or until the cookie is golden brown and the topping is bubbling. Cool in the pan before slicing into bars.

Hazelnut Cheesecake with Chocolate Sauce
Serves 12

This impressive dome-shaped cheesecake has a wonderfully smooth, creamy texture. Begin at least a day ahead to allow the cheesecake to chill thoroughly; it can be prepared up to 3 days ahead and will keep up to 1 week in the refrigerator.

      1 cup hazelnuts
    1½ cups sugar, plus extra for sprinkling
      2 pounds cream cheese, at room
          temperature
      1 cup sour cream
      5 large eggs
     ¼ cup Frangelico or other hazelnut liqueur
      1 teaspoon vanilla extract
        Chocolate Sauce (recipe follows)
        Sweetened whipped cream (optional)

Preheat the oven to 350° F.

Place the hazelnuts on a small cookie sheet and toast in the oven until the nuts are brown and fragrant, about 15 minutes. Cool slightly. Gather the nuts in a dish towel and rub them briskly to remove the skins. Chop coarsely.

Reduce the oven temperature to 325° F. Generously butter the insides of an 8- to 10-cup Pyrex or stainless steel bowl. Sprinkle with sugar; tap out any excess.

Using an electric mixer, beat the cream cheese in a large bowl until smooth. Gradually add the 1½ cups sugar and beat until smooth. Mix in the sour cream. Add the eggs one at a time, beating well after each addition. Fold in the liqueur, vanilla, and hazelnuts and pour the mixture into the prepared bowl.

Place the cheesecake in a deep roasting pan. Pour enough hot water into the pan to come halfway up the sides of the bowl. Bake the cheesecake until it is puffed up and slightly brown on the edges and a knife inserted into the center comes out clean, about 2 hours. Remove from the water and cool at room temperature for 1 to 2 hours. Cover and refrigerate overnight.

Run a small sharp knife around the edge of the bowl to loosen the cake. Fill a slightly larger bowl or the sink with hot water. Dip the bottom of the bowl into the water, letting it stand about 1 minute, or until the cheesecake comes loose from the bowl when lightly shaken.

Invert the cheesecake onto a serving platter; remove the bowl. Smooth the top and sides of the cheesecake with a spatula if necessary. Serve in wedges with chocolate sauce and dollops of sweetened whipped cream, if desired.

Chocolate Sauce
Makes approximately 2 cups

     ½ cup water
      1 tablespoon plus 1 teaspoon instant coffee granules
      1 pound semisweet chocolate, chopped
     ½ cup heavy cream

Bring the water to a boil in a heavy medium saucepan. Remove from the heat; stir in the instant coffee. Add the chocolate and cream. Stir over low heat until the chocolate melts and the mixture becomes smooth. Serve warm.

Note: Well covered, the chocolate sauce can be kept up to 5 days in the refrigerator. Reheat in a double boiler, stirring often.

Wild Blackberry Pie
Serves 6 to 8 (one 9-inch pie)

Each summer Lori and her younger sister stayed with their grandparents in Bremerton, Washington. Grandma always took them berry picking, but they didn't hunt for just any kind of berry. Grandma had a passion for the small seedless blackberry that grow on low scrubby vines—"wild blackber-ries," she called them. During the winters, she would scout for promising patches. Once she found them, she would guard the secret with her life.

Grandma always started her pie just before dinner so it would still be warm for eating. She sliced big pieces into bowls that held the juice and Grandpa would spoon vanilla ice cream over the top.

Pastry

- 3 cups pastry flour, or 2 cups unbleached all-purpose flour and 1 cup cake flour
- 1 tablespoon sugar
- ¼ teaspoon salt
- 1 cup (2 sticks) unsalted butter, chilled Approximately ½ cup ice water, more if necessary

Filling

- 4 cups wild blackberries
- ¾ cup sugar
- 4 tablespoons all-purpose flour
- ½ teaspoon cinnamon
- 2 teaspoons unsalted butter, cut into small pieces
- 1 teaspoon sugar

To make the pastry, blend the dry ingredi-ents together in a mixing bowl. (Grandma always mixed them with a special silver spoon.)

Cut the butter into the dry ingredients with a pastry cutter until the butter is reduced to pea-size bits. Form a well in the center of the flour mixture and add the ice water gradually, until the dough can be gath-ered into a ball. Knead the dough lightly on a floured surface. Cover with plastic wrap and allow the dough to sit at least 10 min-utes to relax the gluten in the flour. (If desired, the dough can be divided into 2 pieces and chilled until needed. Let it soften at room temperature for about 15 minutes or until it becomes pliable enough to roll.)

Preheat the oven to 425° F.

In a large mixing bowl, combine the blackberries, sugar, flour, and cinnamon. Roll out one-half of the pastry and place in a 9-inch pie tin. Spoon the berries into the pie tin and dot with the butter.

Roll out the remaining pastry to cover the top of the pie. Using a sharp knife, cut decorative steam vents in the crust. Set the crust on top of the pie and trim and crimp the edges. Brush the top crust lightly with water and sprinkle it with the sugar.

Bake the pie for 10 minutes, then lower the heat to 375° F. and continue baking until the crust is golden brown and the pie emits a delicious fragrance, about 25 minutes.

Low-Sugar Freezer Jam
Makes about 4½ cups

"This recipe can be doubled, tripled, or made with as many as twenty-seven cups of berries at a time," says Sandi Fein of the Granger Berry Patch. "It uses considerably less sugar than traditional recipes but it still gels nicely."

- 3 cups crushed raspberries, strawberries, boysenberries, blackberries, or marionberries
- 1 package powdered pectin
- 1¾ cups sugar
- 1½ tablespoons (1½ ¼-ounce envelopes) unflavored gelatin

Measure the berries into a 3-quart pan; sprinkle with the pectin. Stir and let stand 30 minutes. Stir in the sugar.

Dissolve the gelatin in ¼ cup boiling water. Bring the berries to a boil over medi-um-high heat, stirring constantly. Remove from the heat and stir in the gelatin. Pour the jam into freezer containers and cool to room temperature. Cover tightly and refrig-erate or freeze.

the CITIES

WO-THIRDS OF THE POPULATION of the Northwest and all but one of its major cities are located in a 500-mile trough situated between the massive volcanic Cascade Range and the range of coastal mountains that stretches from northern California to the spine of Vancouver Island. The string of prominent northwestern cities extends from Ashland and Roseburg in southern Oregon north to Eugene, Salem, and Portland; across the Washington border through Olympia, Tacoma, Seattle, and Bellingham; and finally north to the Canadian cities of Vancouver and Victoria in British Columbia. One hundred sixty miles east of the Pacific, beyond the Cascades, lies the vast Inland Empire, where the major cities are dominated by the commerce of agriculture.

Thousands of years before Europeans and eastern Americans arrived in the Northwest, what are now thriving metropolises were primeval old-growth forests, home to bands of aboriginal Indians. Then, as now, many of the native

inhabitants were economically dependent on trade and commerce, and many of the major northwestern cities were founded on the sites of Indian cultural centers.

Early cities began as a few simple cabins erected along the waterfront or located in the dense forests, with most settlers working in the lumber, fishing, mining, or agriculture industries. In little more than a century, however, these small settlements grew to become some of the busiest seaports on this side of the Pacific Ocean.

Portland, Seattle, and Vancouver, the three major cities of the Pacific Northwest, are bounded by waterways, forests, fertile

farmlands, and the snow-frosted mountains that dominate the horizons from each of the downtown areas. Viewing these spectacular sights while surrounded by freeways, high-rise apartments, and skyscrapers is a continual reminder that just beyond the limits of these bustling cities the wild Northwest still exists.

Prosperity in the form of a ton of Alaska gold, at an estimated worth of two million dollars, came to the Northwest in 1897. Soon thousands from across the country and around the world were flocking to Seattle and ultimately to other northwestern cities to share in the riches to be found in the region. The cities grew rapidly from this point on.

The multicultural tables of the Northwest's cities represent the customs and traditions of its diverse inhabitants, beginning with the ancient aboriginal people. Successive waves of immigrants brought Spaniards, Britishers, Russians, Germans, Scandinavians, Greeks, Italians, East Indians, and Asians to the region. One need only visit any of the downtown farmers' markets to get a taste of the rich cultural stew that comprises these cosmopolitan centers: Stalls offer steaming hot British crumpets, French pastries, Vietnamese spring rolls, Thai curries, Belgian chocolates, hot tamales, and traditional oyster stew.

Home cooks and chefs who live in the Northwest's major cities are extremely fortunate to have access to the highest-quality products available anywhere in the world from both land and sea. Add to this a steady supply of exotic spices, world-class wines, local beers, and distilled spirits and a northwestern city cook has an unlimited palette of ingredients to draw on; city menus are limited only by the imagination of the cook.

Michael and I have spent considerable time in the cities of Portland, Seattle, and Vancouver and we love each of them. Closest to my heart is Seattle, where I was raised. Each summer my family and I picked blackberries and huckleberries under the scorching sun until we were scratched and sunburned. My mother baked the berries

into pies while the kids fought "blackberry wars" using juicy berries as ammunition. We set crawdad traps made of tin cans in the waters of Lake Washington, then dove for our catch just before dinner, often retrieving four-inch-long specimens fished from the docks for salmon and trout. Weekly trips to Pike Place Market in Seattle and other nearby farm markets and U-pick farms kept us well stocked with fresh fish, fruits, and vegetables throughout the summer months.

Later, I worked for many years as a chef in Portland. My days began at five o'clock in the morning when, with a cup of coffee balanced between my legs, I would drive to the market in "Produce Row," where the chattering vendors were just arranging their colorful displays of fruits and vegetables. After selecting the ingredients that most inspired me, I was off to work.

Though his home base is on Orcas Island, Michael spends a fair amount of time in Seattle. When they're in the city, Michael and his family, like many Seattle natives, shop at the Pike Place Market if they're cooking at home. They're also enthusiastic connoisseurs of the city's burgeoning and lively restaurant scene, although on summer evenings Michael is more likely to be found dining on take-out Chinese food in the middle of Lake Union in his kayak. Enjoying the sunset over the city and the distant mountains brings home once again how different the Northwest's cities are from those anywhere else in the country.

The dazzling lights of the Empress Hotel
in Victoria, British Columbia, shimmer in
the waters of the protected harbor.

Ring of Fire: Asian Culinary Influences

Stephen Wong peruses Vancouver's Chinatown; crunchy Tofu Rolls.

WEAVING ASIAN INGREDIENTS LIKE spring ginger, fermented black beans, fresh lychees, and lemongrass through a weft of fresh northwestern foods, chef and restaurateur Stephen Wong creates outstanding "Pacific Rim" dishes. Stephen's wife, Nina, refers to his unique style of culinary alchemy as "cross-over cooking." "He even makes chopsticks out of tree branches when we're out camping," she says.

"Northwest cuisine is not static; it's a cuisine that's continually evolving thanks to all the different cultural influences," says Stephen. When planning a dish or meal, he strives for balance and contrast in flavors, colors, and textures. For example, he'll contrast a creamy chilled soup with a hot, crisp tofu roll or balance rich, oily meats with a lively sweet-and-sour sauce or tangy vinai-

grette. Stephen uses Northwest wines as counterpoints to his dishes as well as to highlight harmonious flavors.

Born and raised in China, Stephen Wong learned the basics of cooking from his family's maidservant. "She had a very holistic approach toward food," he recalls. "Food was medicine to her, and each ingredient she cooked with had a special healing purpose.

"In the Pacific Northwest there is a new emphasis on health and nutrition," says Stephen. "Asian dishes are lighter; they use less meat and lots of fresh vegetables. Asian cooking techniques like steaming, braising, and deep-fat frying lend themselves very well to the foods of the Northwest, allowing foods to maintain integrity without losing freshness and flavor."

Tofu Roll with
Ginger-Plum Compote
Serves 4 (2 rolls each)

Stephen Wong uses tofu skin, the translucent, pliable skin that forms on vats of soybean milk, as a wrapper for these crispy ham and prawn–filled rolls. Tofu skin comes in a variety of styles and is available at most Asian markets. For this recipe, Stephen recommends purchasing frozen tofu skin (it comes in sheets like phyllo dough). Be sure to ask for tofu skin that is made for deep-frying. This can also be used for wrapping dim sum or spring rolls.

- 1 tablespoon vegetable oil
- 1 teaspoon minced garlic
- 2 teaspoons grated fresh gingerroot
- 2 green onions, diced, green and white parts reserved separately
- ½ cup coarsely chopped shiitake or other mushrooms
- ½ cup coarsely chopped ham
- 8 ounces medium-firm tofu, coarsely chopped
- ½ cup fresh prawns or shrimp, shelled and coarsely chopped
- 1 teaspoon cornstarch
- 2 teaspoons soy sauce
- 1 tablespoon water
  Salt and freshly ground black pepper

- 3 to 5 cups peanut oil, for frying
- 2 24-inch round sheets frozen tofu skin, thawed
- 1 large egg, lightly beaten, for egg wash
  Ginger-Plum Compote (recipe follows)

Heat a frying pan or wok over medium-high heat. Add the oil, then stir in the garlic, ginger, the white portion of the green onions, the mushrooms, and the ham. Sauté for 1 minute. Stir in the tofu and continue to cook for about 3 minutes, or until most of the liquid is absorbed. Add the prawns and cook for 1 more minute. Reduce the heat to medium-low.

In a small bowl, mix together the cornstarch, soy sauce, and water. Quickly stir the cornstarch mixture into the tofu mixture, mixing thoroughly. Cook until thickened. Stir in the remaining green onions and season to taste with salt and pepper. Remove the mixture from the heat and set aside to cool slightly.

Heat 3 inches of peanut oil in a heavy saucepan or deep-fat fryer to 360° F. Cut each tofu skin into quarters. Spoon about 2 heaping tablespoons of the filling onto the wide end of each triangle and roll up as you would an egg roll, folding the sides into the roll. Just before finishing the rolling process, brush the tip of each triangle with egg wash so that it will adhere to the roll.

Deep-fry the rolls, 1 or 2 at a time, for about 2 minutes, or until golden. Slice each roll on the diagonal and serve with the plum compote.

Recommended wines: *Pinot Gris, Ehrenfelser*

Ginger-Plum Compote
Makes 1½ cups

- 1½ cups sliced Italian plums (about 2 to 3 large)
- ½ cup white wine
- 2 tablespoons sugar
- 2 teaspoons cider vinegar
- 1 teaspoon grated fresh gingerroot
- ⅛ teaspoon salt
- ⅛ teaspoon freshly ground black pepper

Combine all the ingredients in a nonreactive saucepan. Bring to a boil over medium-high heat and cook for 5 minutes. Set aside to cool. Serve chilled or at room temperature. (This can be prepared up to 2 days in advance.)

Hot Oysters in Beurre Blanc with Cucumber and Swiss Chard
Serves 4

The cool, refreshing lilt of cucumber, and earthy sweetness of Swiss chard accent these silky textured, buttery rich oysters. To prevent oysters from sliding around on the plate, serve on a bed of Swiss chard.

Beurre Blanc Sauce
- 3 tablespoons dry white wine
- 3 tablespoons white wine vinegar
- 1 tablespoon finely chopped shallots
  Pinch of ground white pepper
- 1 tablespoon heavy cream
- ¾ cups (1½ sticks) cold unsalted butter

- ¼ cucumber
- ½ cup finely shredded Swiss chard
- 16 medium Pacific oysters, rinsed

Make the Beurre Blanc: Combine the wine, vinegar, shallots, and pepper in a medium skillet. Bring to a boil and simmer until the liquid has reduced to about ½ tablespoon. Stir in the cream and boil until the cream begins to thicken, about 1 minute. Beat in the butter, bit by bit, keeping the sauce just warm enough to absorb the butter. Strain the sauce and keep warm over hot water in a double boiler or in a thermos.

Peel the cucumber and halve. Use a spoon to scoop out the seeds, then cut the cucumber into fine julienne strips. Combine with the shredded Swiss chard.

Preheat the oven to 400°F.

Just before serving, put the oysters into the hot oven until they start to open, about 10 minutes. Remove and discard the top shells. Place a spoonful of the cucumber/chard mixture on each oyster and top with a spoonful of Beurre Blanc. Serve immediately.
Recommended beverages: *Sparkling wine, Chardonnay*

Prawns on Brown Bread with Homemade Mayonnaise
Serves 4

This is one of the simplest and most delicious appetizers imaginable. Lori first sampled this dish in Ireland at the Ballymaloe Cookery School, where the prawns are served on homemade brown bread. Dense-textured rye bread makes a good substitute.

- 4 slices buttered brown or rye bread
- 4 to 8 leaves butter or oak leaf lettuce
- 20 freshly cooked large (2-inch) prawns
- 3 to 4 tablespoons Homemade Mayonnaise (recipe follows)

  Watercress, flat-leaf parsley, or fennel sprigs
  Lemon slices

Set a slice of buttered bread on each serving plate. Arrange 1 or 2 lettuce leaves on top and place 5 to 6 fat freshly cooked prawns on the lettuce. Pipe or spoon a dollop of mayonnaise on the prawns. Garnish with a sprig of greens and lemon slices.
Recommended wine: *Chardonnay*

Homemade Mayonnaise
Serves 4

- 2 large egg yolks
- ¼ teaspoon salt
  Pinch of dry English mustard or ¼ teaspoon prepared Dijon mustard
- 1 tablespoon white wine vinegar
- 1 cup olive or sunflower oil, or a mixture of the two

Place the egg yolks in a bowl with the salt, mustard, and 1 teaspoon of the vinegar. Place the oil in a measuring cup with a pouring spout. Take a whisk in one hand and the oil in the other. Slowly drip the oil into the yolks drop by drop, whisking constantly. Within a minute you will notice that the mixture is starting to thicken. Once this happens, you can add the oil a little faster, but don't proceed too fast or it will suddenly curdle; yolks can only absorb oil at a certain rate. When all the oil has been added, whisk in the remaining vinegar. Taste and add abit more salt if necessary.

Champagne-Poached Prawns
Serves 2 as a main course

This elegant dish is quick and simple to prepare. Serve the prawns as an appetizer or with bread and a salad as a main course.

2 teaspoons unsalted butter
2 garlic cloves, minced
1½ cups champagne
1 teaspoon dried tarragon, crumbled, or 2 teaspoons fresh
16 large (3-inch) prawns, shelled and deveined

Melt the butter in a large skillet over medium-high heat. Stir in the garlic and sauté about 1 minute, just until it turns golden. Stir in the champagne, tarragon, and prawns, mixing well. Cook just until the prawns turn pink, about 5 minutes. Lift the prawns from the skillet with a slotted spoon and keep warm. Bring the cooking liquid to a boil and simmer for about 5 minutes to reduce slightly. Arrange the prawns on a round platter with a bowl of the poaching broth in the center for dipping.
Recommended wine: *Champagne*

Grilled Scallop Seviche
Serves 4

Chef Vicki McCaffree of Yarrow Bay Grill in Kirkland, Washington, sears plump scallops over a hot grill before marinating them in orange and lime juices. The grilling is optional since the citrus juices do the actual "cooking" of the scallops, but it lends a delicious smoky flavor and golden color to the scallops, which are combined with a colorful salsa of red, yellow, and green peppers, avocado, and fresh cilantro.

1½ pounds large fresh scallops
½ cup fresh lime juice
¼ cup fresh orange juice
1 cup diced mixed red, green, and yellow peppers
1 large avocado, peeled, seeded, and diced
1 serrano or jalapeño chile, minced
4 plum tomatoes or 3 medium tomatoes, seeded and diced
2 tablespoons chopped fresh cilantro
3 tablespoons olive oil
1 teaspoon salt
  Thinly sliced oranges, for garnish
  Fresh cilantro sprigs, for garnish

Thread the scallops onto skewers and grill lightly over a very hot fire, or place under a broiler, just enough to brown the scallops but not enough to cook through.

Remove the scallops from the skewers and place in a nonreactive glass or stainless steel bowl. Pour the lime juice and orange juice over them and marinate them overnight in the refrigerator.

The following day, drain the scallops and place in a clean bowl. Add the peppers, avocado, chile, tomatoes, cilantro, oil, and salt.

To serve, garnish 4 plates with the orange slices and arrange the seviche in the center. Top with fresh cilantro sprigs.
Recommended wines: *Semillon, Sauvignon Blanc, Pinot Gris*

Above and opposite: **Beer-cooked clams.**

Indonesian Peanut Sauce
Makes 1 cup

Sweet, garlicky, and spicy, this thick sauce makes a delicious dipping sauce for steamed clams, roasted duck, chicken, or fish.

  2 *teaspoons vegetable oil*
  3 *tablespoons minced shallots*
1½ *tablespoons minced garlic*
  1 *teaspoon cayenne pepper*
  ½ *cup crunchy peanut butter*
  ¼ *cup water*
  ¼ *cup coconut milk*
  1 *tablespoon lime juice*
  1 *tablespoon soy sauce*
  ½ *teaspoon light brown sugar*

In a skillet, heat the oil over medium heat. Add the shallots, garlic, and cayenne and sauté until fragrant and tender, about 5 minutes. Transfer the sautéed mixture to a food processor or blender; add the remaining ingredients and blend until smooth. Serve at room temperature. Leftovers will keep for 3 or 4 days in the refrigerator.
Recommended wines: *Riesling, Gewürztraminer*

Microbrew Steamers
Serves 6

When a depression hit the fledgling cities of the Pacific Northwest in 1893, many people's meals were suddenly dictated by the tides, giving rise to the expression "When the tide is out, the table is set." City dwellers in Seattle fished from docks for cod and salmon and dug clams and native Olympia oysters from the tide flats. Indian women peddled butter clams along the waterfront streets of Elliott Bay.

The Northwest abounds with microbreweries, all of which brew distinctive, flavorful beers and ales. The yeasty, malty flavor of these brews is an especially good foil for the sweet flavor of steamed clams. Serve these with lots of crusty bread for sopping up the sauce.

  1 *cup (2 sticks) unsalted butter*
12 *garlic cloves, minced*
  1 *teaspoon freshly ground black pepper*
  1 *tablespoon minced shallot*
  ½ *tablespoon chopped fresh tarragon*
  ½ *tablespoon chopped fresh thyme*
  1 *12-ounce bottle northwestern beer, such as Ballard Bitter, Pike Place ale, or Bridgeport's Blue Heron*
  2 *quarts fresh Manila or butter clams, rinsed*
  ½ *cup chopped fresh parsley*
  ½ *cup chopped fresh chives*

In a large pot with a tight-fitting lid, melt the butter over low heat. Add the garlic, pepper, shallot, tarragon, thyme, and beer. Heat to a simmer. Stir in the clams. Cover the pot and steam 4 to 7 minutes, or until all the shells have opened. Sprinkle with the parsley and chives and serve at once.
Recommended beverage: *Microbrewed beer or ale*

Clear Creek Pear Brandy-Cured Gravlax
Serves 10 to 12 as an appetizer

In this Northwest rendition of gravlax, Chef Greg Higgins of Higgins' restaurant uses pear brandy from Portland's Clear Creek Distillery to marinate the salmon. Sliced very thin and served with toasted rye bread and sliced onions, this makes a stunning appetizer. The salmon needs to cure at least 3 days before serving and will keep up to 1 week in the refrigerator.

Dry Marinade
1 cup kosher salt
2 cups packed brown sugar
1 tablespoon black peppercorns
2 tablespoons chopped fresh dill
2 tablespoons coriander seeds
6 bay leaves
6 whole garlic cloves

2 large (1½-pound) fresh salmon fillets, skinned and boned
¼ cup pear brandy or pear eau-de-vie

In a nonreactive mixing bowl, combine the ingredients for the dry marinade, mixing thoroughly. Dredge the bottom of a noncorrosive (glass, ceramic, or stainless steel) pan with half of the dry marinade. Place one salmon fillet on top of the mixture in the pan, then cover the fish with the remaining marinade and top with the remaining fillet. Drizzle the salmon with the pear brandy. Cover the pan with plastic wrap and refrigerate, turning the fish every 12 hours (approximately), for 2 days, spreading the marinade back over the salmon after each rotation.

After 2 days, rinse the fish under cold water and pat dry with paper towels. Separate the fillets and place them on a roasting rack or a cake cooling rack and refrigerate unwrapped overnight. (This allows a bloom to develop on the exterior of the fish.)

Slice the gravlax paper-thin and serve with toasted rye bread.

Recommended wines: *Northwest sparkling wine, Pinot Gris, or ice-cold Clear Creek pear brandy*

Dungeness Crab and Comice Pear Salad with Sesame-Ginger Dressing
Serves 2

Sweet Comice pears and Dungeness crab are an incredible combination—the buttery sweetness of the pear draws out the sweet, rich flavors of the crab.

1 small head of butter lettuce, rinsed and dried
2 ripe Comice pears, peeled and sliced
12 ounces fresh Dungeness crabmeat
Sesame-Ginger Dressing
1 garlic clove, minced
1 teaspoon freshly grated gingerroot
2 tablespoons soy sauce
2 teaspoons sesame oil
2 tablespoons cider vinegar
1 tablespoon minced fresh basil
2 tablespoons sugar

Salt and freshly ground black pepper

Line 2 large salad plates with lettuce leaves. Fan the pear slices over the lettuce and top with the crab. Combine the ingredients for the dressing and drizzle over the salad. Season to taste with salt and pepper.

Recommended wine: *Dry Riesling*

Warm Scallop Salad with Orange and Thyme Dressing
Serves 2

Napped with a light citrus-herb dressing, sea-sweet scallops are set on a colorful bed of purple cabbage, red onions, and leafy greens. This salad makes a quick and healthy meal.

  1 *small head of butter lettuce*
  2 *cups diced escarole*
  ½ *cup chopped cilantro*
  1 *cup finely shredded purple cabbage*
  ¼ *red onion, sliced paper-thin*
  2 *teaspoons unsalted butter or vegetable oil*
 12 *ounces fresh bay scallops*

Orange and Thyme Dressing
  ⅔ *cup fresh orange juice (juice of 2 small oranges)*
  2 *teaspoons grated orange rind*
  1 *teaspoon minced fresh thyme or ¼ teaspoon dried*
  1 *garlic clove, minced*
  2 *tablespoons olive oil*
    Salt and freshly ground black pepper to taste

  1 *green onion, thinly sliced, for garnish*

Wash and dry the lettuce and arrange the leaves on 2 large plates. Scatter the escarole and cilantro over the lettuce, followed by the purple cabbage and red onion.

Melt the butter in a skillet over medium heat. Add the scallops and cook about 5 minutes, or until the scallops are opaque. Spoon the hot scallops and any pan juices over the greens.

Combine all of the ingredients for the dressing in the skillet and return the pan to the stove. Bring the dressing to a boil and pour the hot dressing over the salads. Garnish with the green onion.

Recommended wine: *Dry Riesling*

Warm Dungeness Crab Salad with Hot-Hot Pink Sauce
Serves 2 as a main course

Topped with a stunning hot pink dressing, this salad provides a feast for the eye as well as the palate.

  4 *small beets, peeled, halved, and sliced ¼ inch thick*
  1 *tablespoon white wine or cider vinegar*
  1 *cup shredded butter lettuce*
  1 *cup shredded red oak leaf lettuce*
  2 *large hard-cooked eggs, quartered*
  4 *radishes, sliced*

Hot-Hot Pink Sauce
  1 *cup heavy cream*
  4 *tablespoons sweet pickle relish*
  2 *teaspoons prepared horseradish*
  ¼ *teaspoon salt*
  1 *tablespoon sugar*

  1 *tablespoon unsalted butter*
  8 *to 12 ounces fresh Dungeness crabmeat*
  2 *green onions, sliced diagonally into ¼-inch-thick slices*

Cook the beets in 1 cup of lightly salted water for 10 to 15 minutes, or until tender. Drain, reserving the beet liquid. Sprinkle the beets with vinegar and set aside.

Wash and dry the greens. Tear into bite-size pieces and arrange on 2 large plates. Arrange the hard-cooked eggs, radishes, and beets on top of the greens.

Combine the reserved beet juice, cream, relish, horseradish, salt, and sugar in a saucepan and bring to a boil. Continue to boil for about 5 minutes, or until the sauce is slightly thickened.

Heat the unsalted butter in a skillet over medium-low heat. Add the crab and sauté until it is just warmed through. Spoon the crab over the salads. Top with the pink sauce and garnish with the green onions.

Recommended wines: *Pinot Blanc, Merlot*

Shrimp and Artichoke Heart Pizza
Serves 4 as an appetizer

Puréed artichokes cooked with onions and garlic make a thick, savory sauce for this shrimp and red pepper-topped pizza invented by Maria Lara and Bob Mingus, friends of Michael and Jeanne. The dough is very easy to make, but the topping would be just as delicious on a storebought pizza base.

Dough for 1 12-inch pizza

1 small onion
2 garlic cloves
   Olive oil, as needed
1 6½-ounce jar marinated artichoke hearts
   Salt and freshly ground black pepper
1 red bell pepper
1½ cups shredded mozzarella cheese
12 medium shrimp, peeled and deveined
½ cup freshly grated Parmesan cheese

Preheat the oven to 475° F.

Spread the pizza dough out on a greased 12-inch pizza pan to make a thin crust. Set the dough in a warm place and let it rise while preparing the topping.

Coarsely chop the onion and garlic. Heat 2 tablespoons of the olive oil in a skillet over medium heat; add the onion and sauté until soft, about 5 minutes. Add the garlic and cook 1 minute. Stir in the artichoke hearts together with their marinade and cook until heated through, about 7 minutes. Transfer the ingredients to a blender and puree until smooth. Add salt and pepper to taste.

Slice the red pepper into ⅛-inch round slices. Spread the artichoke puree evenly over the dough and sprinkle with the mozzarella cheese. Distribute the red pepper slices decoratively over the pizza and place 2 shrimp inside each slice. Sprinkle the

Parmesan cheese on top and drizzle lightly with olive oil.

Bake the pizza on the lowest oven rack (preferably on a pizza stone or tiles) for about 25 to 30 minutes. The crust should be brown and the topping bubbling hot. Serve immediately.

Recommended beverages: *Cabernet Sauvignon, Merlot, or microbrewed beer or ale*

Pizza Dough
Makes one 12-inch pizza

1 teaspoon (⅓ packet) active dry yeast
1 teaspoon sugar
½ cup warm water
3 tablespoons olive oil
¾ teaspoon salt
2 cups unbleached all-purpose flour (approximately)

Combine the yeast and sugar in a mixing bowl. Pour in the water and set aside for about 5 minutes, until dissolved. Stir in the olive oil, salt, and flour, ½ cup at a time, until the mixture forms a soft ball.

Turn the dough onto a floured surface and knead for about 5 minutes, incorporating more flour as needed to form a smooth dough. Place the dough in an oiled mixing bowl; cover with plastic wrap and let rise at room temperature until doubled in bulk, about 1½ hours.

Punch down the dough and press it onto an oiled 12-inch pizza pan. Let the dough rise for 20 minutes before adding toppings.

Scallops in Basil Sauce
Serves 2

The mild licorice flavor of fresh basil is a wonderful complement to the sea-sweet meat of the Northwest's scallops. Steamed asparagus makes a delicious side dish.

> 1 tablespoon unsalted butter
> 1 garlic clove, minced
> ¼ cup diced onion
> ¼ cup dry white wine
> ½ cup fish or chicken stock
> 1 tablespoon minced fresh basil or 2 teaspoons dried, crumbled
> 1 teaspoon light brown sugar
> 1 pound large scallops, rinsed, drained, and blotted dry
> ½ cup half-and-half

Melt the butter in a large skillet over medium heat. Add the garlic and onion and cook about 5 minutes, until the onion is transparent but not browned. Stir in the wine, fish stock, basil, and brown sugar, then add the scallops and simmer for about 5 minutes, or until they are no longer opaque. Using a slotted spoon, remove the scallops from the pan and keep warm.

Add the half-and-half to the poaching liquid and bring the sauce to a boil. Simmer rapidly for about 10 minutes, or until the sauce is the consistency of heavy cream. Strain the sauce through a sieve into a mixing bowl, add the scallops, and toss to coat thoroughly. Serve warm.

Recommended wines: *Sauvignon Blanc, Chardonnay*

Salmon in Zucchini Blossoms
Serves 4

At The Herbfarm, owner Ron Zimmerman cooks tender chunks of fresh salmon inside golden zucchini blossoms, allowing the delicate herbal flavor of the flowers to permeate the fish.

Pick the zucchini blossoms in the morning, before the heat of the day. Blossoms can be stored upright in the refrigerator with their bases in a glass of water until needed.

> 1½ pounds salmon fillets
>   Salt
>   Cayenne pepper
> 8   zucchini blossoms, with or without the zucchini attached
> 6   tablespoons (¾ stick) unsalted butter
> 2   shallots, minced
> 2½ tablespoons fresh lime juice
> 3   tablespoons dry white wine
> 5   basil leaves
> 3   tablespoons heavy cream
>   Olive oil
> 3   tablespoons finely diced zucchini

Remove any small bones from the salmon fillets with small pliers or tweezers. Trim off all fat and divide the salmon into 8 pieces, each about 1 × 2 inches. Season the salmon with a little salt and a touch of cayenne.

Using a small knife, remove the stamens from the zucchini blossoms. Carefully insert one piece of salmon into each blossom and set aside.

Melt 1 tablespoon of the butter in a skillet; add the shallots and sauté over low heat until translucent, about 5 minutes. Stir in the lime juice, wine, and 2 whole basil leaves. Simmer the mixture slowly until it has reduced to about 2 tablespoons, about 5 minutes. Discard the basil leaves. Add the cream and bring the sauce to a boil. Remove from the heat and set the sauce aside.

Preheat the oven to 350° F.

Paint the stuffed blossoms lightly with olive oil and place them on a lightly greased baking sheet. Bake for 12 minutes, or until the salmon is just cooked through.

Meanwhile, return the sauce to the heat and bring to a boil. Turn off the heat. Using a wire whisk, stir in the remaining 5 tablespoons of butter 1 tablespoon at a time. Season to taste with salt and cayenne pepper. Roll the remaining 3 basil leaves into a small bundle and snip with scissors into fine strands, letting them fall into the sauce. Stir in the diced zucchini.

Nap each serving plate with about ¼ cup of the sauce and place 2 stuffed blossoms on each plate.

Recommended wines: *Pinot Gris, Chardonnay*

Warm Skate Wing with Coriander Sauce
Serves 4

Lori learned to prepare this dish at the Ballymaloe Cookery School in Ireland, where many of the same fish and shellfish found in the Northwest abound. Skate, a member of the ray family, has a broad flat body with triangular wings, which are the edible part. The meat has a delicate sweet flavor that pairs well with vinegar-based sauces. It is also delicious poached and served with hollandaise sauce.

1 medium skate wing (about 1½ pounds)
1 onion, chopped
¼ cup chopped fresh parsley
2 tablespoons rice wine vinegar or cider vinegar
Pinch of salt

Sauce

2 tablespoons balsamic or sherry vinegar
¼ cup olive oil
2 tablespoons sunflower or peanut oil
Salt and freshly ground black pepper to taste
½ teaspoon Dijon mustard
1 teaspoon coriander seed
1 tablespoon chopped green onions or chives, sliced at an angle
1 rounded tablespoon diced red onion

Place the skate wing in a pan wide enough for the fish to lie flat. Cover the wing completely with cold water; add the onion, parsley, vinegar, and salt. Bring the water gently to a boil. Let the skate simmer for 15 to 20 minutes, or until just cooked through. Lift the skate out of the water and place on a dish or board. Carefully remove the skin and the large cartilaginous piece of bone and divide into 4 portions.

Meanwhile, make the sauce by combining the balsamic vinegar, oils, salt, pepper, and mustard. Heat the coriander seed for a few minutes in a dry skillet until fragrant, then crush in a mortar and pestle and add to the dressing. Just before serving, stir in the green and red onions.

Spoon the sauce over each warm skate portion.

Recommended wines: *Dry Gewürztraminer, sparkling wine*

Above: **Fresh herbs make this dressing sing.**
Opposite: **A simple but stunning salad.**

Market Greens with Jimmy Beard's Dressing
Serves 6

"Jim Beard was a teacher and stylist with a great palate," says Christina Orchid of Christina's on Orcas Island. "He loved simple foods with the distinctive flavors of themselves. He especially believed that good salad greens should be barely touched with flavor."

 1 *head of red oak leaf lettuce*
10 *stems arugula*
10 *stems bok choy*
10 *stems mustard greens*
20 *stems mâche*
 1 *small bunch of pepper cress*
 1 *head of Bibb lettuce*

 1 *cup good olive oil*
⅓ *cup mild red wine vinegar*
 2 *tablespoons chopped fresh herb of choice:*
    chives, chervil, parsley, or marjoram
    Salt and freshly ground black pepper
    to taste

Wash and dry the greens. Tear into pieces and combine in a large salad bowl. Whisk together the olive oil, vinegar, herbs, and salt and pepper. Drizzle over the salad and toss well. Serve immediately.

Yakima Asparagus Salad
Serves 6

Contrary to what many people believe, thick fat asparagus spears are actually juicier and more flavorful than pencil-thin asparagus. Search them out the next time you're in the market.

 1 *red onion*
 1 *red bell pepper*
 1 *yellow bell pepper*
 1 *tablespoon balsamic vinegar*
 3 *tablespoons extra virgin olive oil*
    Freshly ground black pepper
    Kosher salt
30 *large thick asparagus spears, trimmed*
 6 *ounces finely grated Parmesan cheese*
    (about 2 cups)

Preheat the oven to 375° F. Place the unpeeled onion in a pie tin and roast for 30 minutes. Add the red and yellow peppers and cook 15 minutes more. Remove the vegetables from the oven and let cool until they can be handled. Peel the onion and slice it into very thin rings. Peel and seed the peppers; slice thinly. Place the vegetables in a mixing bowl.

Whisk together the vinegar, olive oil, pepper, and salt to taste; pour over the vegetables, mixing well. Let sit 1 hour to overnight.

Steam the asparagus for 6 to 8 minutes, or until it is bright green and tender but still toothsome. Rinse under cold running water to stop the cooking process.

Fan the asparagus into a sunburst on a serving platter. Spoon some of the pepper-onion mixture between each asparagus spear. Dust with grated cheese. Serve at room temperature.

Recommended wine: *Sauvignon Blanc*

Christina's Roast Lamb with Spinach and Feta
Serves 8 to 10

Lamb has been popular in the Northwest since it was introduced in the early 1800s. This rather elegant presentation is quick to prepare, especially if you have the butcher butterfly the lamb for you.

1 *4 to 6 pound leg of lamb, boned and butterflied*
1 *tablespoon salt*
1 *tablespoon freshly ground black pepper*
15 *fresh spinach leaves, well-washed and stems removed*
8 *ounces feta cheese, cut into ½-inch cubes*
3 *red bell peppers, roasted, peeled, seeded, and cut into 1-inch strips*

Preheat the oven to 350° F.

Spread the butterflied leg of lamb on a work surface with the smoother side down. Rub the cut surface with 1½ teaspoons of the salt and 1½ teaspoons of the pepper. Arrange the spinach leaves over the lamb, covering the entire surface. Place the chunks of feta cheese in a lengthwise strip down the middle of the lamb, then top with the roasted red pepper strips. Roll the lamb tightly, starting from one long edge, enclosing the filling completely. Secure with butcher's twine or skewers and season the roast with the remaining salt and pepper.

Place the lamb on a rack in a roasting pan, seam side down, and roast for about an hour, or 15 minutes per pound. Let the lamb rest for 20 minutes before slicing.

Recommended wines: *Pinot Noir, Merlot*

Peppered Beef Tenderloin with Corn and Chile Pudding
Serves 6

This robustly flavored roast is wonderful at room temperature or thinly sliced for open-faced sandwiches.

The golden corn pudding is studded with chiles and Jack cheese. It also makes a delicious accompaniment to chicken or pork.

Corn and Chile Pudding

   8 *ears corn*
 ½ *cup chopped roasted Anaheim peppers (about 2 whole)*
1 ½ *cups grated Jack cheese*
 ½ *cup minced onion*
   1 *chipotle chile, minced (optional)*
   2 *tablespoons all-purpose flour*
   3 *large eggs*
 ½ *cup buttermilk*

Peppered Roast Beef Tenderloin

   3 *tablespoons cracked peppercorns (preferably a mix of red, black, white, and green)*
   1 *tablespoon large crystal sea salt*
2 ½ *pounds fillet of beef, trimmed*

Opposite: **The tender lamb's filling is visible in each serving.** *Above:* **R**are beef and corn pudding are an unbeatable combination.

Preheat the oven to 350° F.

Make the corn and chile pudding: Using a sharp knife, scrape the corn off the cobs into a large bowl. Add the peppers, 1¼ cups cheese (reserve ¼ cup for topping), onion, and the chipotle, if using. In a small bowl, whisk together the flour, eggs, and buttermilk. Stir into the corn mixture. Butter a 2-quart casserole dish. Pour the mixture into the dish and bake for about 45 minutes. Top with the remaining cheese and bake about 15 more minutes, or until the pudding is firm and slightly pulled away from the edges of the dish. Keep warm.

Raise the oven temperature to 450° F.

Place the peppercorns between 2 sheets of wax paper and crush with a rolling pin or the back of a large knife. Transfer the peppercorns to a large platter. Add the salt and mix well. Roll the beef in the peppercorn mixture until completely coated, pressing the peppercorns firmly into the meat.

Place the beef in a roasting pan and cook for 10 minutes. Reduce the heat to 350° F. and continue cooking for 10 more minutes, or until the beef is medium rare (120° F. on an instant-read thermometer). Let the meat sit 10 minutes before slicing.

Recommended **wines**: *Cabernet Sauvignon, Merlot*

Veal with Chestnuts, Lemon, Apples, and Roasted Garlic
Serves 4

Rich with the flavors of garlic, apples, lemon, and rosemary, this makes a savory entrée for a chilly winter evening. Cooked cabbage dressed with a little butter and cream rounds out the meal beautifully.

- 2 *pounds veal leg or shoulder, approximately 1½ inches thick, sliced into individual serving portions*
- 1 *head of garlic, separated into cloves and peeled (see Note)*
- 2 *tablespoons olive oil*
- 1 *3-inch fresh rosemary sprig or 1 tablespoon dried*
- 1¼ *cups whole chestnuts, shelled, or 1 10-ounce can, drained*
- 2 *apples, peeled, cored, and quartered*
- 1⅓ *cups chicken or veal broth*
  - *Grated rind of 1 lemon*
  - *Freshly ground black pepper*

Preheat the oven to 375° F.

In a large ovenproof skillet, brown the veal and garlic cloves in the oil over medium-high heat for about 10 minutes. Remove from the heat. Scatter the rosemary, chestnuts, and apple slices around the veal, then pour the chicken broth over the veal. Sprinkle with the lemon rind, season to taste with pepper, cover, and bake for about 40 minutes, or until the meat is tender and thoroughly cooked.

To serve, place a portion of veal on each serving plate. Spoon some of the chestnuts, apples, and garlic around the veal and drizzle some of the warm pan juices over all.

Note: A simple method of peeling garlic is to pinch the pointed ends of each clove between your thumb and index finger until the papery skin splits open.

Recommended wines: *Zinfandel, Merlot, Pinot Noir*

Polenta Lasagna
Serves 4

Portland sausage maker Fred Carlo seasons his spicy Italian sausage with fennel, fresh garlic, and dried red chiles, letting the mixture sit overnight to marry the flavors. Served with a simple green salad, warm bread, and a hearty red wine, few things taste better on a cold, rainy winter evening.

Polenta
- 6 *cups cold water, or more if necessary*
- 1½ *cups coarse cornmeal*
- ½ *cup (1 stick) unsalted butter*
- ¾ *cup freshly grated Parmesan cheese*
  - *Salt*

- 2 *tablespoons olive oil*
- 8 *Italian sausage links*
- 1 *large onion, diced*
- 3 *garlic cloves, minced*
- 2 *tablespoons minced fresh basil*
- ½ *cup dry red wine*
- 15 *fresh plum tomatoes, cored and diced, or 2 pounds canned Italian tomatoes, crushed*
- 1½ *cups freshly grated Parmesan cheese*
- 6 *ounces mozzarella cheese, preferably fresh, crumbled or grated*

To make the polenta, combine the cold water and cornmeal in a heavy saucepan. Cook the mixture over low heat, stirring often, until the polenta is thick and no longer feels grainy on your tongue, adding more water if necessary. Stir in the butter, Parmesan cheese, and salt to taste. Cover and keep warm.

Make the lasagna: In a heavy skillet, heat the olive oil over medium heat. Prick the sausages with a fork and brown them in the oil until cooked through. Drain the sausages on paper towels. When cool enough to handle, slice ½ inch thick and set aside. In the same skillet, sauté the onion, garlic, and

Pike Place Market

NO MATTER WHEN YOU visit the Pike Place Public Market in downtown Seattle, the air vibrates with passionate energy as farmers, fishmongers, meat cutters, and more, many of whom carry on third-generation traditions, display and market their goods. Established in 1907, Pike Place Market is America's oldest farmers' retail market. The downtown waterfront location is believed to have been used as a trading area by Northwest Indians.

Thomas P. Revelle, a law school graduate from the University of Washington, was known as the "father" of the market. He made a study of public markets dating back to ancient days and determined that the best way to save consumers money was to cut out the middleman and allow growers to sell directly to consumers. His brainchild quickly prospered.

Many Italian immigrants set up stalls in the market, including Giuseppe (Joe) Desimone, an Italian immigrant born in 1880, who was known as the "king" of the Pike Place Market. Joe stowed away aboard a ship bound for America at the age of seventeen, landing on Ellis Island with just forty dollars. From there he headed to the Northwest where, his uncle had told him, "vegetables grew like weeds."

Antonio Ditore arrived in Seattle in 1902 at the age of twenty-four and began peddling vegetables door to door. Later he opened his own vegetable market on Broadway.

Pasqualina Verdi, one of Seattle's best-loved vendors, moved to the states in 1950 from her family's farm in Avellion, Italy. Pasqualina married Seattle farmer Dominic Verdi and joined him at the market in 1956. Her son, Mike, and his wife, Sue, carry on the family tradition.

Many of the market's first merchants were Sephardic Jews who came to Seattle from the Isle of Rhodes or southern Turkey. Many are still active in the market, including Sol Amon and his brother Irving, and Harry Calvo and Cookie Cohen, who work at the Pure Food Fish Market, which was started in 1911. The Levys' City Fish Market was started in 1918 by David Levy, one of the first Sephardic Jews to move to Seattle.

Asian truck farmers were integral to the market from its inception. These enterprising individuals, with their expert gardening skills, turned small garden plots into profitable businesses. After the bombing of Pearl Harbor in 1942, all Japanese in the Seattle area were forced into prison camps. This, combined with the birth of supermarkets, nearly led to the demise of the market.

Fortunately the "Seattle spirit" persevered. The Pike Place Market was renovated in the 1970s and continues stronger than ever, with a string of successful businesses like Emmett Watson's cozy Oyster Bar; DeLaurenti's Specialty Foods, offering regional and imported specialties; the Pike Place Brewery and Liberty Malt Supply Company; and the original Starbucks coffee shop, which opened in 1971.

basil over low heat for about 15 minutes, or until the onion is golden. Deglaze the pan with the red wine, then add the tomatoes and cook the sauce over low heat for 45 minutes to 1 hour, stirring occasionally.

Preheat the oven to 350° F.

To assemble the lasagna, spoon one-third of the polenta in the bottom of a 9 × 13-inch baking dish. Top with half of the tomato sauce, half of the sausage, and one-third of the cheeses. Repeat for a second layer and top with a third layer of polenta topped with grated cheese. Bake the lasagna for about ½ hour, or until hot and bubbly.

Recommended wines: *Cabernet Sauvignon, Merlot*

Cappuccino Cheesecake
Serves 12

This rich, espresso-flavored cheesecake is the house specialty at Christina's Restaurant on Orcas Island. Chef/owner Christina Orchid recommends letting the cheesecake chill overnight. If you like, top the cheesecake with 1 cup of sour cream sweetened with 2 tablespoons of sugar and 1 tablespoon of Kahlúa as it cools.

Chocolate Cookie Crust
  1   9-ounce package chocolate wafer cookies
  ½   cup sugar
  1   teaspoon cinnamon
  1   tablespoon unbleached all-purpose flour
  ½   cup (1 stick) unsalted butter, melted

Cheesecake
  2   pounds cream cheese, softened
  2   cups sugar
  1   tablespoon unbleached all-purpose flour
  1   teaspoon vanilla extract
  4   large eggs
  ¼   cup heavy cream
  2   tablespoons instant espresso granules
  1   tablespoon Kahlúa or coffee liqueur

Preheat the oven to 350° F.

Place the chocolate cookies in a food processor or blender and grind until fine crumbs are formed. Add the sugar, cinnamon, and flour and combine thoroughly. Add the butter and pulse once or twice to mix. Turn the crumb mixture into a 10-inch springform pan and pat down firmly to cover the bottom of the pan. Chill the crust for at least 10 minutes.

Meanwhile, beat the cream cheese with the sugar in a large mixing bowl until the mixture is smooth and silky. Add the flour and vanilla, mixing well. Beat in the eggs one at a time, mixing thoroughly after each addition. Heat the ¼ cup cream to scalding and stir in the instant espresso until dissolved. Spoon one-third of the cream cheese mixture

into a separate mixing bowl and whisk in the espresso mixture and the Kahlúa.

Spoon half of the plain cream cheese mixture into the springform pan, smoothing the top with a spatula. Top with the espresso mixture, then cover with the remaining cream cheese mixture. Tap the pan gently on the counter to settle the filling. Place the cheesecake in a large roasting pan filled with enough warm water to come 2 inches up the sides of the springform pan. Bake for 1½ hours, then turn off the oven and let the cheesecake cool in the oven for at least 1½ hours or until a toothpick inserted in the center comes out clean. Chill thoroughly before unmolding and slicing.

Gewürztraminer Ice
Serves 12

Flavored with a spicy Northwest Gewürztraminer, this golden ice makes a refreshing palate cleaner between courses.

  1   cup water
  1   cup sugar
  1   bottle Gewürztraminer wine, chilled
      Juice of 1 lemon
      Mint leaves and edible flowers, for
      garnish

Combine the water and sugar together in a saucepan. Bring to a boil, uncovered, and boil for 1 minute. Remove the syrup from the heat and chill thoroughly.

Stir the wine and lemon juice into the cold syrup. Pour the mixture into a 9 × 13-inch baking pan and set the pan in the freezer. Once ice crystals begin to form around the edges of the pan (about 2 hours), run a whisk around the edges of the pan to break them up. Continue whisking every hour or so until the entire pan is frozen into crystals. To serve, scoop the ice into small goblets and garnish with edible flowers and mint leaves.

Chocolate-Chestnut Pâté with Coffee Custard Sauce
Serves 10

In this elegant, simple-to-prepare dessert, dark chocolate and pale chestnut mousses are swirled together and molded in a loaf pan. After chilling, thick slices of pâté are set in a coffee custard sauce. Chestnut puree can be purchased at most specialty food stores, or you can make your own by pureeing freshly roasted, shelled chestnuts. This dessert will keep up to 4 days in the refrigerator.

> ¾ cup (1½ sticks) unsalted butter, at room temperature
> ¾ cup sugar
> 4 large egg yolks
> 1 teaspoon vanilla extract
> 3 tablespoons brandy
> 1 16-ounce can unsweetened chestnut puree
> 6 ounces good-quality white chocolate, chopped
> 12 ounces bittersweet or semisweet chocolate, chopped
> 1¼ cups chilled heavy cream
> Coffee Custard Sauce (recipe follows)

Line a 9 × 5 × 3-inch loaf pan with plastic wrap. Using an electric mixer, cream the butter and sugar in a large bowl until light and fluffy. Beat in 2 egg yolks, mixing thoroughly. Mix in the vanilla and brandy.

Using an electric mixer, beat the chestnut puree in another large bowl until smooth. Beat in half of the butter mixture. Melt the white chocolate in the top of a double boiler over simmering water, stirring until smooth. Cool slightly. Beat the white chocolate into the chestnut mixture.

Melt the bittersweet chocolate in the top of a double boiler over simmering water, stirring until smooth. Cool until just warm to the touch, about 20 minutes. Mix the bittersweet chocolate into the remaining butter mixture. Beat in the remaining 2 egg yolks.

Whip the cream until it forms soft peaks. Whisk one-third of the whipped cream into the bittersweet chocolate mixture to lighten it, then gently fold in the remaining whipped cream.

Drop about one-third of the chestnut and bittersweet chocolate mousses into the prepared pan in alternating dollops. Run a small sharp knife through the mousses to create a marbleized pattern. Repeat the process with the remaining mousse. Cover the pâté with plastic and chill until firm, about 4 hours.

To serve, invert the pâté onto a plate and remove the plastic. Heat a long thin knife under warm water; wipe dry. Cut the pâté into 10 slices, cutting straight down (do not use a back-and-forth motion) and wiping the knife between each cut. Serve the pâté with a generous spoonful of Coffee Custard Sauce.

Coffee Custard Sauce
Makes about 3 cups

> 1 tablespoon hot water
> 1 tablespoon instant coffee granules
> 2 cups half-and-half
> ½ cup sugar
> 4 large egg yolks
> 1 teaspoon vanilla extract

Combine the hot water and instant coffee in a small bowl, stirring until the coffee has dissolved. Scald the half-and-half in a medium saucepan; remove from the heat. In a medium bowl, beat the sugar and egg yolks to blend. Gradually whisk in the hot half-and-half. Return the mixture to the saucepan and stir over low heat until the mixture thickens slightly and coats the back of a spoon, about 5 minutes. Strain into a medium bowl. Stir in the coffee mixture and vanilla and refrigerate until well chilled.

Bourbon-Walnut Torte with Brown Sugar Whipped Cream
Serves 10

Walnut orchards thrive in the Northwest, and in the fall you can glean your own walnuts from the orchards for a minimal price. Freshly harvested nuts are much more flavorful than any we've ever purchased from a store. Here walnuts and bourbon, two flavors with a remarkable affinity for each other, are combined in a moist, rich torte that is filled and frosted with a fluffy whipped cream frosting flavored with brown sugar and bourbon.

Torte
3¼ cups walnuts (about 13 ounces)
¼ cup unbleached all-purpose flour
2 teaspoons baking powder
¼ teaspoon ground nutmeg
½ teaspoon salt
6 large eggs, separated
2 cups granulated sugar
¼ cup bourbon whiskey

Whipped Cream Frosting
1¼ cups firmly packed light brown sugar
¼ cup bourbon whiskey
3 cups chilled heavy cream

2 tablespoons bourbon whiskey, for assembly

Walnut halves, for garnish

Make the torte: Position a rack in the center of the oven and preheat to 350° F. Butter and flour 2 10-inch springform pans.

Finely grind the walnuts in a food processor or blender, being careful not to overprocess. Transfer the walnuts to a large mixing bowl and with a wire whisk, mix in the flour, baking powder, nutmeg, and ¼ teaspoon salt.

Using an electric mixer, beat the egg yolks and 1 cup of the granulated sugar in a large bowl until doubled in volume and a wide ribbon forms when the beaters are lifted, about 5 minutes. Stir in the bourbon, then fold into the nut mixture.

Using an electric mixer fitted with clean dry beaters, beat the egg whites and remaining ¼ teaspoon salt in another large bowl until soft peaks form. Gradually beat in the remaining 1 cup of granulated sugar and continue beating until stiff peaks form. Gently fold the whites into the pecan mixture in 2 or 3 additions.

Divide the batter between the prepared pans. Bake until a toothpick inserted into the center comes out clean, about 35 minutes. Cool the torte layers in the pans for 15 minutes, then release the pan sides and invert the layers onto a rack. Remove the pan bottoms. (These can be prepared 1 day ahead. Cover tightly with plastic wrap.)

Make the frosting: Combine the brown sugar and the ¼ cup of bourbon in a large bowl. Stir until the mixture is smooth. Gradually beat in the cream. Continue beating until stiff peaks form.

Assemble the torte: Place 1 torte layer on a cake platter. Brush with 1 tablespoon bourbon. Spread about 2 cups of frosting over the torte. Top with the second torte layer. Brush with the remaining 1 tablespoon bourbon. Spread the top and sides of the torte decoratively with the remaining frosting. If desired, reserve ½ cup of frosting. Spoon into a pastry bag fitted with a large star tip. Pipe decoratively around the edges of the torte. Garnish the edges of the torte with walnut halves.

Clear Creek Distillery

WHILE TRAVELING IN EUROPE, *native Oregonian Stephen McCarthy of Portland's Clear Creek Distillery became enchanted with French pear brandy. When he learned that the Bartlett pears grown on his family's Hood River orchards were the same as those used to produce France's famous Poire Williams, McCarthy decided to try his hand at a Northwest version.*

McCarthy studied distilling in France, Switzerland, and Germany before purchasing his copper Alsatian still. Unobtrusively located in an old warehouse in northwestern Portland, Clear Creek Distillery is one of the few copper-pot distilleries operating within the United States.

The distillation process evaporates liquid from a fruit mash by boiling it. As the steam condenses, the alcoholic vapor is trapped and saved, a process that concentrates and captures the essential flavors of the fruit in unsweetened spirits, or eaux-de-vie. "What you get in a bottle of brandy is pure condensed essence of fruit, and that's about it," says McCarthy.

He has gained international recognition for the exceptional quality of his eau-de-vie de poire (pear brandy), as well as apple brandy (produced from golden Delicious apples), kirsch (cherry brandy), framboise (raspberry eau-de-vie), plus grappas and marcs, spirits produced from the pomace left after a wine pressing.

McCarthy's pear brandy is rich and buttery. Although it's not sweet, it exudes the spicy fragrance and voluptuous fruit of ripe Bartlett pears. Traditionally eau-de-vie is served as an after-dinner drink with coffee or espresso on the side. On cold wintry nights, McCarthy likes a touch of apple or pear brandy in his coffee, and to break the heat on hot summer nights he suggests freezing a bottle of pear brandy in a block of ice, like vodka, and drinking it ice cold.

Stephen McCarthy ages his pear eau-de-vie in glass carboys, *opposite;* apple brandy is aged in Limousine oak barrels to add complexity to the flavor. *Above:* Stephen inspects the **Bartlett** pear crop.

Chocolate Brandy and Hazelnut Tart
Makes one 10-inch tart or one 9-inch pie

Ninety-eight percent of the hazelnuts raised in the United States are grown in Oregon's Willamette Valley; the other two percent come from southwestern Washington. Oregon hazelnuts are world renowned for their extremely large size and exceptional flavor. Though hazelnuts are native to the temperate regions of the Northern Hemisphere, including the Pacific Northwest, the nuts of the wild hazels indigenous to the Northwest are quite small; the hazelnuts favored for cultivation are of the European species (*Corylus maxima* and *Corylus avallena*), which produce much larger nuts. This tart filling is as thick and chocolaty as fudge.

- 1 recipe Sweet Tart Pastry
- ¼ cup (½ stick) unsalted butter, softened
- ¾ cup firmly packed brown sugar
- 3 eggs, at room temperature
- 12 ounces bittersweet or semisweet chocolate, melted and cooled to room temperature
- ¼ cup brandy
- ¼ cup unbleached all-purpose flour
- 1 cup chopped toasted hazelnuts
  Garnish
  Confectioners' sugar
  Sweetened whipped cream (optional)

Line a 10-inch tart pan or 9-inch pie tin with the pastry. Trim the pastry, leaving ½ inch overhanging the edges of the pan. Fold under and crimp. Chill the pastry at least 15 minutes, or until needed.

Preheat the oven to 350° F.

In a mixing bowl, cream together the butter and sugar until fluffy. Add the eggs one at a time, beating well after each addition. Mix in the melted chocolate, incorporating thoroughly. Add the brandy and flour, then fold in the hazelnuts. Pour the filling into the prepared tart shell and bake about 25 minutes, or until a toothpick inserted in the center comes out clean. (Don't be alarmed if the filling puffs up like a soufflé; it will sink down as it cools.)

Let the tart cool to room temperature. Dust with confectioners' sugar and serve with sweetened whipped cream, if desired. **Recommended wine:** *Port*

Berry Compote with Pear Eau-de-Vie
Serves 4 to 6

In the Northwest, a profusion of wild berries is available during the summer months. You can substitute any of your favorite fruits in this recipe—cherries, peaches, or grapes, for example, are all delicious drenched in pear brandy.

- 1 cup blackberries
- 1 cup golden raspberries
- 1 cup blueberries
- ¾ cup pear eau-de-vie
  Sugar to taste
  Mint leaves for garnish

Combine the berries and pear brandy in a large bowl, mixing well. Add sugar to taste, if necessary. Cover with plastic wrap and let the fruit marinate for at least ½ hour. Garnish with mint leaves. Serve chilled or at room temperature.

Browned Butter Pear Tart
Makes one 10-inch tart

In this elegant dessert, a sweet cookie crust is filled with a golden browned butter custard and sweet juicy pears. Fat-bottomed Comice pears are Lori's favorite; Bartlett and Bosc pears are also delicious. If desired, the pastry and custard can be prepped 1 to 2 days ahead and the tart assembled just before baking. This recipe also works beautifully with tart apples; simply substitute cinnamon for the nutmeg in the custard. For an extra finishing touch, brush the cooled tart with melted apricot jam.

- ¾ cup (1½ sticks) unsalted butter
- 3 large eggs, at room temperature
- 1 cup sugar
- 6 tablespoons unbleached all-purpose flour
- ½ teaspoon ground nutmeg
- 1 recipe Sweet Tart Pastry

- Juice of ½ lemon
- 4 to 5 large ripe pears
- ¼ cup sugar
- Sweetened whipped cream (optional)

In a small saucepan over medium heat, melt the butter, then continue to cook until the butter is golden brown. Meanwhile, whisk the eggs in a mixing bowl to blend. Gradually whisk in the sugar and flour and mix until thickened. Whisk in the nutmeg. Add the hot butter to the egg mixture very gradually, whisking constantly. Chill the custard for 1 hour to thicken.

Roll out the sweet tart pastry and line a greased 10-inch tart pan. Trim the edges, leaving ½ inch overhanging the rim of the pan. Fold under and crimp. Chill the pastry until firm, about 15 minutes.

Preheat the oven to 350° F.

Squeeze the lemon juice into a large, non-reactive mixing bowl. Peel, core, and slice the pears crosswise into ¼-inch-thick slices.

Pour the chilled custard into the tart shell, smoothing the top. Starting at the outer edge of the tart, pack the pear slices tightly in concentric, overlapping rings, ending in the center of the tart. Sprinkle the tart with ¼ cup sugar.

Bake for about 35 minutes, or until the custard is golden brown and a knife inserted in the center comes out clean. Serve at room temperature with sweetened whipped cream, if desired.

Recommended wines: *Late-harvest Riesling, Gewürztraminer*

Sweet Tart Pastry
Makes one 10-inch pastry shell

This is Lori's favorite pastry for fruit tarts; it's as sweet and buttery as shortbread. These instructions are for blending the pastry by hand, but it can also be made successfully in a food processor or in a mixer fitted with a paddle attachment.

- 1¾ cups unbleached all-purpose flour
- ¼ cup sugar
- 10 tablespoons chilled unsalted butter, divided into ½-inch pieces
- 2 large egg yolks
- ½ teaspoon vanilla extract
- Cold water, as needed

Combine the flour and sugar in a mixing bowl. Cut in the butter with a pastry blender until it is reduced to pea-size bits. Make a well in the center of the flour and add the egg yolks and vanilla, mixing well. Knead lightly to form a stiff dough, adding a bit of cold water if necessary to bring it together. Cover the dough with plastic wrap and let sit 10 minutes to relax the gluten.

Note: If desired, the pastry can be chilled or frozen at this point and brought to room temperature before using.

Nowhere in the country are coffee-based drinks
more widely or enthusiastically consumed.
From left to right: frothy cappuccino;
a "double tall" caffe latte; classic espresso; iced
mochaccino; potent espresso macchiato.

Sleepless in Seattle

The Northwest's tremendous thirst for coffee was partially quenched in 1971, when Starbucks opened its first store at Seattle's Pike Place Market. Since then, Starbucks has grown to a multimillion-dollar operation, with sidewalk stands and retail stores operating throughout the Northwest. That was just the beginning. Now, on nearly every corner of the city, in every convenience store, and in every theater, coffee—in every shape and form—is offered. In Seattle, one radio station has even renamed the freeway express lanes, "the espresso lanes."

No matter where you go in the Northwest, in large cities and small towns alike, someone is "Krups-ing the java," offering Northwesterners their favorite beverages—lattes, tall and short; espresso; mocha; café au lait, and more—with perhaps a cookie or two on the side.

Orange-Hazelnut Biscotti
Makes 36 cookies

    4 cups unbleached white flour
    1 tablespoon baking powder
    ½ teaspoon salt
    1 cup unsalted butter
 1½ cups sugar
 1½ orange zest (white pith removed) finely
      chopped
    2 eggs
    2 tablespoons brandy
    1 tablespoon orange liqueur
    1 cup toasted hazelnuts (page 82)

In a small bowl, stir together the flour, baking powder, and salt and set aside. In a large mixing bowl, cream together the butter, sugar, and orange zest. Add the eggs and beat until well blended. Add the brandy and orange liqueur and mix well. Stir in the dry ingredients until just blended. Stir in the nuts.

Roll the dough into a log, 1 inch high and 2 to 3 inches wide. Bake in a 325° F. oven for 25 minutes until lightly browned. Cool the log for about 10 minutes. Slice on the diagonal into ½-inch cookies. Return cookies to the baking sheet to a 300° F oven and lightly toast them for 10 minutes on each side. Cool the cookies completely before storing. In an airtight container, the biscotti will keep for a month.

Variation: Add ½ cup mini semisweet chocolate chips

Anne's Lemon Walnut Meltaways
Makes 36 cookies

This delightful cookie was created by Anne Garfield for Rose's Bakery on Orcas Island. Try them with a warming caffe latte or cappuccino.

    ½ cup (2 sticks) unsalted butter
    1 cup sugar
    1 ounce lemon juice
 1½ teaspoon lemon extract
    1 tablespoon lemon zest (white pith removed)
      finely chopped
    2 cups unbleached white flour
    ½ teaspoon salt
    ½ cup cornstarch
    1 cup chopped walnuts

In a mixing bowl, cream together the butter and sugar. Add the lemon juice, lemon extract, and lemon zest to the butter and sugar and mix well. Add the the flour, salt, cornstarch, and walnuts to the mixture and continue to mix until all of the ingredients are thoroughly combined.

Roll the dough into a log of whatever shape you desire and wrap it well in plastic wrap. Chill the log several hours until the dough is firm. Slice the log into cookies approximately ⅓ inch wide and arrange them on a cookie sheet. Bake the cookies in a 350° F to 375° F oven 10 to 12 minutes or until they are brown around the edges.

Mocha Latte

Serves 1

This is what it takes to get Lori going every morning.

    1 teaspoon cocoa powder
    1 teaspoon sugar
    2 teaspoons hot tap water
    ½ cup of milk
    ½ cup freshly brewed espresso coffee

In a small saucepan combine the cocoa powder and sugar. Stir in the hot water, mixing well. Place the mixture over medium heat and bring to a boil. Pour in the milk and heat to scalding, whisking constantly. Remove from the heat and set aside. Simultaneously pour the hot cocoa and the espresso into an expresso bowl or large coffee cups.

Espresso Ice Cream Soda

Serves 2

This revs your engine like a jump-start on a warm summer afternoon. Serve it with long iced-tea spoons and straws for scooping and sipping.

    ¾ cup freshly brewed espresso coffee
    ¼ cup sugar
    ½ cup milk
    1 cup coffee ice cream
      Soda water, as needed

Add the sugar to the freshly brewed coffee and stir to dissolve. Chill until cooled to at least room temperature. Stir in the milk.

Fill 2 tall glasses halfway with the coffee mixture. Add a scoop of coffee ice cream to each glass. Top with soda water.

Peach Daiquiris

Serves 4

When friends drop by during the summer months to visit Mary and Fred McCulloch at their Seattle houseboat, they often blend up a pitcher of daiquiris made with fresh Yakima peaches. They serve this frosty concoction in wide-rimmed champagne glasses.

    2 fresh peaches, unpeeled, sliced
    ½ cup frozen lemonade concentrate
    12 large ice cubes (approximately)
    4 jiggers dark rum

Place the peaches, lemonade, and ice cubes in a blender or food processor. Blend until the ice is crushed. Place 1 jigger of rum in each wide-rimmed champagne glass. Top with the peach mixture and stir.

MOUNTAINS
and
FORESTS

MUCH OF THE MYSTERY, power, and grace of the Pacific Northwest lies in its mountain ranges, alive with icy-blue glaciers, fiery volcanoes, and lush evergreen forests.

The Cascades, one of the northwestern United States's major mountain chains, extend from the Feather River region of northeastern California through Oregon and Washington to the Fraser River in British Columbia. With a summit elevation of over 8,000 feet in the northern and central portions of the range, the Cascades form an important climatic and economic barrier between the eastern and western portions of the Pacific Northwest. When moist Pacific storms reach the mountains, the air masses cool, resulting in plentiful rains. The western slope of the Cascades, with more than eighty inches of precipitation yearly, is densely canopied with Douglas fir, red cedar, hemlock, and other evergreens. The eastern flank, which receives just ten to twenty-five inches of rain

per year, is a semiarid desert, sparsely vegetated with tall slender pines and chaparral, including sagebrush, tumbleweed, and dry grasses.

A number of conical-shaped volcanoes, which were formed in relatively recent times, tower above the general level of the Cascades. These include Mount Baker near the Canadian border, which occasionally steams and spurts; Mount Rainier; and the recently erupted Mount St. Helens. Farther south lie Mount Adams, Mount Jefferson, Mount Pitt, Mount Scott, and Mount Shasta, in northern California.

On clear days the majestic snow-frosted peaks of the Olympic Mountains dominate Seattle's western skyline. Located within the Olympic National Forest, these mountains of northwestern Washington are bounded on three sides by water—the Pacific Ocean, the Strait of Juan de Fuca, and Puget Sound. Receiving 142 inches of rainfall annually, this unique rain forest is one of the most lush wildlife ecosystems on earth. Dripping with moisture, imposing forests of giant ferns, Douglas fir, hemlock, red cedar, Sitka spruce, and pine symbiotically support long, flowing strands of moss, lichen, and sapro-phytic plants.

For hundreds, probably thousands, of years, coastal Indians had walked through the Cascades near Snoqualmie pass during the summer months to trade with people who lived on the eastern slopes of the mountains. Later, Hudson's Bay fur trappers used the same paths. After several aban-doned attempts to establish a road linking east to west, a wagon road was finally built in 1868, linking the new cities of Olympia, Tacoma, and Seattle with the interior.

High above the timberline, vegetation is sparse, with only a few gnarled and stunted alpine firs, mountain hemlocks, sedges, and grasses breaking the rugged terrain. When one descends in elevation, the vegetation becomes thick and lush as it nears sea level. Wild life, including Roosevelt elk, deer, cougar, coyote, black bear, raccoon, mink, otter, beaver, mountain goat, skunk, marmot, and many birds, abounds in these forested areas, providing northwesterners with wild game throughout the year.

Deep in the damp forests, thick layers of leaves and evergreen needles decompose softly into the earth, providing rich habitats for earthy-flavored mushrooms, including Matsutake, *Boletus edulis*, morels, and apri-cot-scented chanterelles. A profusion of wild berries, including huckleberries, blue-berries, and blackberries, grows in the forests, and many alpine lakes and streams are filled with trout.

Although meals in the mountains and forests are often simple affairs—cooked over an open fire or in a rustic cabin over a small stove—cooks in the Northwest are masters at turn-ing the wild foods of these regions into tempting dishes.

For centuries wild game has been served with tangy wild berry sauces, which serve as the perfect counterpoint to the rich, robust flavors of game. In the spring and fall a bounty of wild mushrooms makes delicious soups, sauces, or ragouts. The wild mushrooms also are delicious just brushed with olive oil and grilled over a fire. High mountain lakes and streams abound with trout, which are delectable smoked over cedar or alder. Smoked or jerked meats, such as bear, elk, and deer, are also regional favorites.

Desserts are usually straightforward—fresh or preserved wild berries cooked into juicy cobblers or pies. Wild plums, crab apples, and elderberries all make delicious preserves for dessert or breakfast.

Michael and I spent much time camping, hiking, and skiing in the mountains and forests of the Northwest. No matter where we were, the highlight of the day was the evening meal. Whether dining simply on canned beans and stick-roasted hot dogs or on more elaborate fare like barbecued veni-son or panfried trout, food never tasted bet-ter than when we were seated around a crackling fire under the open skies.

Foraging

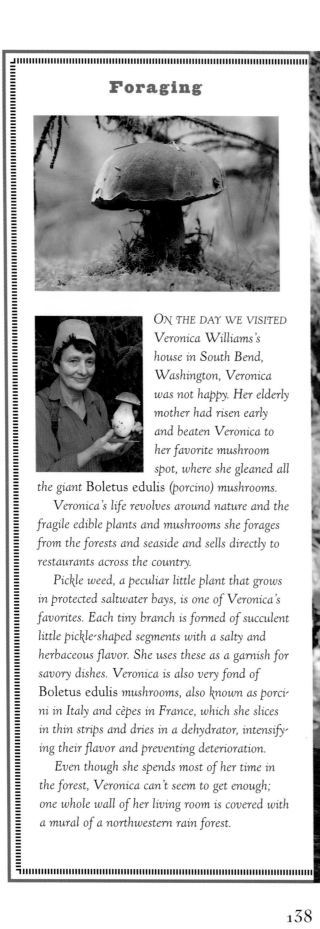

ON THE DAY WE VISITED *Veronica Williams's house in South Bend, Washington, Veronica was not happy. Her elderly mother had risen early and beaten Veronica to her favorite mushroom spot, where she gleaned all the giant* Boletus edulis *(porcino) mushrooms.*

Veronica's life revolves around nature and the fragile edible plants and mushrooms she forages from the forests and seaside and sells directly to restaurants across the country.

Pickle weed, a peculiar little plant that grows in protected saltwater bays, is one of Veronica's favorites. Each tiny branch is formed of succulent little pickle-shaped segments with a salty and herbaceous flavor. She uses these as a garnish for savory dishes. Veronica is also very fond of Boletus edulis *mushrooms, also known as porcini in Italy and cèpes in France, which she slices in thin strips and dries in a dehydrator, intensifying their flavor and preventing deterioration.*

Even though she spends most of her time in the forest, Veronica can't seem to get enough; one whole wall of her living room is covered with a mural of a northwestern rain forest.

Blackberry Sour Cream Coffee Cake
Serves 6 to 8

Filled with juicy blackberries, this moist sugary coffee cake is delicious for breakfast or an afternoon snack.

> ½ cup (1 stick) unsalted butter, softened
> 1 cup sugar
> 2 eggs
> 1 cup sour cream
> 2 cups sifted unbleached all-purpose flour
> 1 teaspoon salt
> 1 teaspoon baking powder
> 1 teaspoon baking soda
> 1 teaspoon vanilla extract
> 1 cup blackberries or huckleberries
>
> **Topping**
> ¼ cup unsalted butter, softened
> ½ cup firmly packed light brown sugar
> ½ teaspoon cinnamon

Preheat the oven to 350° F. Grease and flour an 8-inch square baking pan.

In a mixing bowl, cream together the butter and sugar at high speed until pale and fluffy. Add the eggs one at a time, beating thoroughly after each addition. Add the sour cream, beating until smooth. Sift together the flour, salt, baking powder, and baking soda and add to the egg mixture. Add the vanilla and blend thoroughly. Fold in the blackberries.

In a small bowl, combine the ingredients for the topping. Pour half of the batter into the prepared pan and sprinkle with half of the topping mixture. Add the remaining batter and sprinkle with the remainder of the topping mixture. Bake approximately 35 minutes, or until a toothpick inserted in the center comes out clean.

Cascade Mountain Snow Pancakes
Makes about 6 4-inch pancakes

Snowflakes are tiny, feathery, geometric ice crystals formed from water vapor in the air. When they collect on the ground, air is trapped between them. When this airy snow is incorporated into a thick pancake batter, it leavens the batter in much the same way as beaten egg whites would. It is important to use only fresh, powdery snow in this recipe, or the pancakes won't rise. Also, make sure all the other ingredients are cool.

> ¾ cup unbleached all-purpose flour
> 1 teaspoon baking powder
> 2 teaspoons sugar
> ½ teaspoon salt
> 2 teaspoons vegetable oil
> ½ cup milk
> ½ cup fresh huckleberries or blueberries (optional)
> ½ cup freshly fallen snow

Sift together the flour, baking powder, sugar, and salt. Gradually add the oil and milk, stirring vigorously to make a thick, smooth batter. Fold in the berries, if using. Quickly fold in the freshly fallen snow. Drop by ¼-cupfuls onto a hot greased griddle or skillet. Fry on both sides until golden, about 5 minutes. Top with butter and warm maple syrup.

Yogurt Huckleberry Muffins
Makes 12 muffins

These low-fat, huckleberry-studded muffins are delicious with tea or coffee.

6 tablespoons (¾ stick) unsalted butter, softened
1 cup plus 2 tablespoons sugar
3 large eggs
2 cups sifted unbleached all-purpose flour
½ teaspoon baking soda
¼ teaspoon salt
1 cup plus 2 tablespoons plain yogurt
½ teaspoon vanilla extract
1½ cups huckleberries or blueberries

Preheat the oven to 425° F. Grease a 12-cup muffin tin.

In a mixing bowl, cream together the butter and sugar until pale and fluffy. Add the eggs one at a time, mixing well. Sift together the flour, baking soda, and salt. Add the flour mixture to the egg mixture in 3 additions, alternating with the yogurt. Stir in the vanilla and huckleberries.

Fill each muffin cup two-thirds full with batter. Bake about 15 minutes, or until cooked through.

Blackberry-Apple Breakfast Crepes
Serves 4

Loragene Gaulin loves preparing these fruit-filled crepes for breakfast. She picks the berries early in the morning so they're as fresh as possible. "I get suited up in rain gear and gum boots and, clutching my bowl, I can reach the hard-to-get places and fill the bowl in minutes," she says. "Our guests at the Roberts Creek Country Cottage Bed and Breakfast get a real thrill out of freshly picked wild blackberries." Loragene serves thick slices of Canadian back bacon or ham with these crepes.

Crepes
1 large egg, lightly beaten
1 cup milk
¼ cup unbleached all-purpose flour
½ teaspoon baking powder
⅛ teaspoon salt

Blackberry-Apple Filling
4 tablespoons (½ stick) unsalted butter
1 cup sugar
4 cups fresh or frozen blackberries
4 medium apples, cored, peeled, and sliced
Juice of ½ lemon

Sour cream or plain yogurt
Blackberries, for garnish

Make the crepes: Beat together the egg, milk, flour, baking powder, and salt in a mixing bowl or 4-cup measuring cup. Heat a crepe pan or well-seasoned oiled cast-iron frying pan over medium heat. Add a few drops of vegetable oil and spread evenly over the bottom of the pan. Pour in just enough batter to cover the bottom of the pan. Turn and rotate the pan so the crepe mixture spreads out evenly and thinly. Cook for about 1 minute, or until the bottom of the crepe is golden. Gently flip the crepe and cook until golden on the second side. Transfer the crepe to a plate. Continue making crepes, stacking them on top of each other, until the batter is used up.

Make the filling: Melt the butter in a large skillet. Stir in the sugar, blackberries, apples, and lemon juice. Sauté the fruit over medium heat until the apples are tender, then reduce the heat and simmer until the sauce has thickened, about 15 minutes.

Assemble crepes: Lay one crepe on a warm plate. Spoon blackberry-apple filling over one half of the crepe and top with a spoonful of sour cream or yogurt. Fold over the crepe and garnish with several spoonfuls of the filling and a few whole blackberries. Allow 2 crepes per serving.

Wild Mushroom Omelet with Pesto Cream Sauce
Serves 2

A visitor to the home of David Campiche and his wife, Laurie Anderson, during mushroom season is likely to find a whole refrigerator stocked with edible mushrooms they have gathered from the Long Beach Peninsula on the southern Washington coast.

"Beginning late summer, if there's some rain, and there usually is, we can collect chanterelle mushrooms. The season extends to the first freeze, usually in November, during which we gather twenty to thirty varieties of edible mushrooms, which we often serve for breakfast," says David.

Pesto is available in many grocery stores and delis or you can make your own.

2 teaspoons unsalted butter
1 garlic clove, minced
6 ounces wild mushrooms (chanterelles, Boletus edulis, morels, or lobster mushrooms, for example), wiped clean and diced into ¼-inch pieces
3 tablespoons diced red onion
3 tablespoons diced red bell pepper
2 tablespoons brandy
2 tablespoons prepared basil pesto
¼ cup heavy cream
   Salt and freshly ground black pepper to taste
6 large eggs

Heat the butter over medium heat in a large skillet. Add the garlic and cook about 2 minutes, or until golden. Stir in the mushrooms, onion, and red pepper and cook, stirring often, for about 3 minutes, or until slightly softened. Pour in the brandy and ignite with a match, allowing the alcohol to burn off. (The flame will extinguish itself.)

Stir in the pesto and the cream. Simmer the sauce for several minutes, until it is thick and creamy. Add salt and pepper.

Meanwhile, beat the eggs lightly. Preheat an omelet pan or nonstick skillet over medium heat. Brush the pan lightly with butter or oil. Pour the eggs into the pan and reduce the heat to low. Using a spatula, lift the edges of the omelet from the sides of the pan and tip the pan to allow the runny center of the omelet to flow underneath. Repeat this a few times, until the eggs are just barely firm, about 7 minutes.

Fill the omelet with the mushroom filling, fold over, and serve warm.

Recommended wine: *Pinot Noir*

143

Spring Vegetable Pâté with Watercress and Fiddlehead Ferns
Serves 6

Cheri Walker of the Shoalwater Restaurant in Seaview, Washington, adapted this recipe from *The New Basics Cookbook* by Julee Rosso and Sheila Lukins to incorporate Northwest fiddlehead ferns. Fiddleheads are the newly sprouted shoots of young ferns, most commonly Lady Fern, or Bracken Fern, both of which were eaten by natives of the North Coast. When steamed, these fiddle-heads have the texture and taste of aspara-gus with more complex woodsy flavor notes.

   2 *large leeks*
   1 *tablespoon unsalted butter*
   4 *carrots, peeled and cut into ¼-inch dices*
   1 *bunch watercress, stems removed*
   6 *ounces fiddlehead ferns*
   1 *cup cooked long-grain rice*
  ½ *cup chopped green onions*
   2 *tablespoons chopped fresh fennel*
   1 *teaspoon salt*
    Freshly ground black pepper to taste
   1 *tablespoon cornstarch*
   4 *large eggs*
 1¼ *cups half-and-half*
    Fresh Tomato Sauce (recipe follows)

Preheat the oven to 350° F. Grease the sides and bottom of a 9 × 5 × 3-inch loaf pan. Trim the leeks, leaving about 1-inch of green. Halve the leeks lengthwise and rinse well. Cook them in boiling water for about 4 minutes, or until soft. Drain and pat dry.

Melt the butter in a skillet. Add the car-rots and cook over medium heat, stirring occasionally, until soft, about 8 minutes. Transfer the carrots to a large bowl. Cook the watercress in the same skillet, adding a little more butter if neccessary, for about 2 minutes, or just until it begins to wilt.

Drain, squeezing out excess moisture, and finely chop the watercress, adding it to the carrots.

Bring 2 cups of water to a boil and add the fiddlehead ferns. Cook about 4 minutes, or until they are tender. Drain the ferns and add them to the carrots and watercress. Stir in the rice, green onions, fennel, salt, and pepper. Sprinkle the cornstarch over the vegetables and stir until it has been absorbed.

Beat the eggs and half-and-half together until smooth. Stir this into the vegetables and mix thoroughly. Pour the mixture into the prepared pan, and then place the pan in a larger baking dish filled with 1 inch of hot water.

Bake the pâté about 1 hour and 10 min-utes or until a knife inserted in the center comes out clean. The top should be dry and firm. Chill the pâté for several hours before unmolding.

Place a serving dish on top of the pâté and invert. Slice the pâté into ¾-inch-thick slices and spoon tomato sauce on the side. If desired, garnish with fresh cucumber and a sprig of fresh fennel.

Recommended wines: *Sparkling wine, Sauvignon Blanc*

Fresh Tomato Sauce
Makes 1 cup

   4 *ripe plum tomatoes, quartered*
  ½ *large cucumber, peeled, seeded, and cut into ¼-inch dice*
   1 *tablespoon minced fresh chives*
   1 *tablespoon chopped fresh fennel or dill*
    Salt and freshly ground black pepper to taste

Combine the tomatoes, cucumber, chives, fennel or dill, and salt and pepper in a food processor or blender and process until smooth.

Oregon Blue Cheese Pear
Serves 6 to 8

Molded into the shape of a fresh pear, this cheesy blend makes an impressive appetizer, yet it takes only minutes to prepare. Serve with fresh fruit or crackers.

½ pound cream cheese, softened
½ pound Oregon blue cheese

In a mixing bowl, beat the cream cheese until smooth. Crumble the blue cheese into the cream cheese and fold in gently with a wooden spoon or rubber spatula. Lay a sheet of plastic wrap on the counter and spoon the cheese mixture into the center of the plastic. Lift each corner of the plastic up to envelop the cheese; with your hands, mold the cheese into a pear shape. Chill at least 1 hour or overnight until set.

To serve, peel off the plastic wrap. If desired, press the stem from a fresh pear into the top of the blue cheese pear for garnish.

Recommended wine: *Pinot Noir*

Morels on Toast
Serves 2 to 4 as an appetizer

Spring morels (*Verpa Bohemica*) grow under cottonwood trees along the shores of the Columbia River in early spring. They are delicious sautéed in butter and garlic and served on sourdough toast.

2 tablespoons unsalted butter
1 garlic clove, minced
8 2-inch-long morels, cleaned and diced
½ teaspoon sugar
  Salt to taste
2 tablespoons olive oil
4 small slices sourdough bread

In a saucepan over medium heat, heat the butter and garlic until bubbly. Add the mushrooms and cook about 5 minutes, or

until soft. Stir in the sugar and add salt; set aside. In a separate skillet, heat the olive oil over medium heat; add the bread and fry until golden on both sides. Top with the warm morels.

Recommended wines: *Sauvignon Blanc, Pinot Noir*

Sautéed Chicken Livers and Matsutake Mushrooms
Serves 2

Matsutake mushrooms (*Armillaria ponderosa*) are big fleshy, cream-colored mushrooms that are prevalent in the pine forests of the Northwest. The mushrooms, which are highly prized by the Japanese, have an unmistakable peppery odor and flavor similar to that of fresh horseradish; they are great with the creamy, earthy flavor of tender chicken livers.

2 tablespoons olive oil
2 garlic cloves, minced
1 small onion, diced
2 large Matsutake mushrooms, wiped
  clean and sliced
12 ounces chicken livers, rinsed

In a large skillet, heat the olive oil over medium heat. Sauté the garlic and onion until golden, about 5 minutes. Add the mushrooms and cook 5 more minutes, stirring often. Add the chicken livers and cook until they are just cooked through, about 12 minutes.

Recommended wines: *Cabernet Sauvignon, Merlot*

Northwest-style Shrimp-Stuffed Baguettes
Serves 8

For picnics, Pauli Schoomaker of Portland, Oregon, prepares these sandwiches ahead of time and wraps them in butcher paper. Several large, choice cold-water shrimp are found in Pacific waters. These include spot shrimp (found from California to Alaska) and the sidestripe and coonstripe shrimp of the Pacific Northwest and Alaska.

¾ pound cooked, peeled shrimp, rinsed
1 small cucumber, peeled, quartered lengthwise, and sliced
6 radishes, quartered and sliced
1½ tablespoons chopped fresh dill
⅓ cup mayonnaise, preferably homemade
Juice of ½ lemon
Salt and freshly ground black pepper to taste
2 12-inch-long loaves of French bread
10 yellow pear tomatoes, halved
10 cherry tomatoes, halved

Combine the shrimp, cucumber, radishes, and dill in a mixing bowl; add the mayonnaise and lemon juice and combine gently. Season with salt and pepper.

Slice the bread lengthwise, leaving one side attached to act as a hinge. Pull most of the bread out of the loaves and discard, leaving the crust shells. Pack the cavity of the bread with the shrimp mixture. Stud this with the tomatoes, embedding them in the shrimp mixture. Close the sandwiches and wrap tightly with butcher paper or plastic wrap. Tie the rolls together with strings of raffia spaced about 2 inches apart and chill. To serve, slice through the paper with a sharp knife to make individual sandwiches.

Recommended wines: *Muller Thurgeau, Riesling*

Marinated Albacore Tuna Sandwich
Serves 8

Prepare the filling for these tasty sandwiches with fresh or canned tuna.

12 ounces fresh albacore tuna
½ red onion
2 teaspoons black peppercorns
Basil Marinade
¼ cup Parmesan cheese cut into 1-inch chunks
1 cup fresh basil leaves
¼ cup fresh oregano
1 tablespoon Dijon mustard
2 tablespoons red wine vinegar
⅔ cup olive oil
½ teaspoon freshly ground black pepper
Salt to taste

½ cup each red, yellow, and green bell peppers, cut lengthwise into 2-inch strips
¼ cup chopped kalamata olives
½ cup thinly sliced Walla Walla or red onion
2 large hard-cooked eggs, chopped
1 tablespoon capers, drained
2 12-inch-long loaves of French bread

Fill a pot with enough cold water to cover the fish. Add the red onion and peppercorns. Bring the liquid to a simmer and add the tuna. Simmer about 6 to 7 minutes. Test the fish with a fork; it should flake easily. Drain and cool.

Make the basil marinade. In a food processor or blender, reduce the cheese to fine bits. Add the basil and oregano and process for about 10 seconds. Add the mustard and vinegar, then add the oil in a slow steady stream. Add pepper and salt. Reserve ⅓ cup marinade and set aside.

Break the tuna into chunks in a large

Above and right: **W**rapped in sturdy butcher paper and tied with raffia, these tasty sandwiches are just right for backpacking or picnicking.

mixing bowl. Add the peppers, olives, and onions. Pour the marinade over the tuna and vegetables, mixing well, and let the mixture marinate in the refrigerator for at least 2 hours to blend the flavors.

Assemble the sandwiches according to the directions for Northwest-style Shrimp-Stuffed Baguettes. Sprinkle the tuna mixture with the chopped eggs and capers, then sprinkle with the reserved marinade before wrapping.

Recommended wines: *Semillon, Sauvignon Blanc*

147

Sagebrush Biscuits
Makes 12 biscuits

Sagebrush or bitter brush (*Purshia tridentata*) grows wild in many parts of the United States from New Mexico up through Montana and Washington. The leaves have a complex spicy and musty flavor similar to that of saffron, which can substitute for the wild sage. The secret to turning out tender biscuits is to work quickly, handling the dough as little as possible.

> 3½ *cups unbleached all-purpose flour*
> 2 *tablespoons baking powder*
> 1 *teaspoon salt*
> 3 *tablespoons sugar*
> 1 *tablespoon dry crumbled sagebrush*
> *leaves or* ½ *teaspoon saffron threads*
> *soaked in 1 teaspoon boiling water*
> ½ *cup (1 stick) unsalted butter, chilled*
> 1½ *cups heavy cream*

Preheat the oven to 425° F.

Into a large mixing bowl, sift together the flour, baking powder, salt, and sugar. Stir in the crumbled sagebrush leaves or saffron, mixing well.

Using a pastry blender, cut the butter into the flour mixture until it has the texture of coarse cornmeal. Make a well in the center of the dry ingredients and pour in the cream all at once. Working quickly, stir the mixture with a spatula just long enough to moisten all of the dry ingredients.

Turn the dough out onto a floured surface and knead very lightly for about 30 seconds. Divide the biscuit dough into 2 portions. Roll or pat each portion into a rectangle about ¾ inch thick. Using a round biscuit cutter, divide each portion into 6 equal biscuits. Place the biscuits about 1 inch apart on an ungreased baking sheet. Bake for 12 to 15 minutes, or until golden. Serve warm.

Salal Berry Quick Bread
Makes 1 loaf

Salal berries (*Gaultheria shallon*), members of the heath family of plants, which includes blueberries and huckleberries, were highly regarded by the indigenous people of the Northwest, who devised special black mountain-goat horn spoons (which resisted berry stains) just for consuming them.

The berries have a sweet blueberry flavor with a refreshing minty aftertaste; substitute cultivated blueberries if salal does not grow in your area.

> 6 *tablespoons (¾ stick) unsalted butter,*
> *softened*
> ½ *cup sugar*
> 1 *large egg, at room temperature*
> 1 *cup unbleached all-purpose flour*
> ½ *teaspoon salt*
> 1 *teaspoon baking powder*
> 1 *cup milk*
> 1 *cup salal berries or blueberries*

Preheat the oven to 350° F. Lightly oil a 4½ × 8½-inch loaf pan.

In a mixing bowl, cream the butter. Add the sugar, beating at high speed until pale and fluffy. Reduce the speed and add the egg, mixing thoroughly.

In another mixing bowl, blend together the flour, salt, and baking powder with a wire whisk. Add the dry ingredients and the milk to the butter mixture alternately in 3 batches, beginning with the flour, mixing well after each addition. Fold in the salal berries.

Pour the prepared batter into the pan and bake about 50 minutes, or until a toothpick inserted into the center of the loaf comes out clean.

Let the bread cool 15 minutes in the pan, then turn out onto a cooling rack. Serve warm or let cool to room temperature. Store in the refrigerator up to 3 days.

Wild Greens and Alpine Strawberry Salad with Strawberry-Peppermint Vinaigrette
Serves 4

Alpine strawberries (*Frageria bracteata*) grow wild in the mountains and forests of the Pacific Northwest. They are also cultivated at places like the Glorious Garnish and Seasonal Salad Company in Aldergrove, British Columbia, where partners Susan Davidson, Dave McCandless, and Heather Pritchard raise an assortment of organic produce. Gary Faessler, of the "Chefs About Town" cooking show in Vancouver, British Columbia, sprinkles this colorful salad with bee pollen (available at health food stores), which adds a distinctive taste and crunch.

If you don't have alpine strawberries, substitute *fraises des bois* or chopped larger berries. The dressing calls for Strawberry Vinegar, which needs to be prepared ahead.

Dressing
- 1 teaspoon honey
- ¼ cup Strawberry Vinegar
- 1 teaspoon chopped fresh peppermint
- 1 teaspoon Dijon mustard
- 1 teaspoon finely minced shallots
- ⅓ cup safflower oil
- 2 tablespoons walnut oil

- 8 cups mixed greens, herbs, and edible flowers
- 24 red or white alpine strawberries, hulled
- 1 tablespoon bee pollen

Place the honey, vinegar, peppermint, mustard, and shallots in a mixing bowl. Slowly whisk in the safflower and walnut oils. Divide the salad greens among 4 plates and top with the strawberries. Drizzle the dressing over the salad and sprinkle with bee pollen.

Strawberry Vinegar
Makes 1 quart

- 1 cup fresh strawberries, washed and hulled
- 2 cups white wine vinegar

In a nonreactive saucepan, mash the strawberries with a potato masher. Add the vinegar and bring to a simmer over medium heat. Remove from the heat and let cool to room temperature. Strain into clean, dry bottles. Store at room temperature up to 3 months.

Note: For Blueberry Vinegar, substitute 1 cup blueberries for the strawberries. This recipe can be doubled.

Salal Relish
Makes approximately 2 cups

This relish is fantastic with grilled venison or any kind of game bird.

- ½ cup sugar
- 2 cups salal berries or blueberries
- 1 cup water
- 1 onion, finely diced
- 1½ cups cider vinegar
- 1 garlic clove, minced

In a medium saucepan, combine the sugar, salal berries, and water. Bring to a boil over medium-high heat, then reduce the heat and simmer until the berries begin to soften, about 10 minutes. Remove the pan from the heat and immediately stir in the onion, vinegar, and garlic. Let the relish sit at least 15 minutes before serving to blend the flavors. Serve warm or at room temperature. This will keep up to 1 week stored covered in the refrigerator.

Above: **Great picnic fare, the beans need no refrigeration; the striking potato salad,** *opposite.*

Garden Beans in Blueberry Vinaigrette
Serves 6 to 8

The Blueberry Vinegar adds a lovely sweetness to this simple dish.

1/2 *pound young green beans*
1/2 *pound fresh yellow wax beans*
1 *tablespoon minced shallot*
1 *teaspoon prepared Dijon-style mustard*
1 *tablespoon Blueberry Vinegar (page 149)*
4 *tablespoons olive oil*
  Salt and freshly ground black pepper
    to taste

Rinse the beans and snip off their stem ends. In a large saucepan, bring 1 1/2 quarts of water to a boil, add the beans, and cook for 1 minute. Drain the beans and plunge immediately into cold water. Drain again and set aside.

In a small bowl, combine the shallot, mustard, and vinegar, mixing thoroughly with a wire whisk. Gradually whisk in the olive oil and add the salt and pepper. Place the drained beans in a mixing bowl and toss with the vinaigrette. Chill for 2 hours before serving.

Purple Peruvian and Yellow Finn Potato Salad
Serves 6 to 8

Allow this colorful salad to marinate overnight in the refrigerator.

1 *pound purple potatoes, halved and*
  sliced 1/4 inch thick
1 *pound yellow finn potatoes, halved and*
  sliced 1/4 inch thick

1 *garlic clove, minced*
1 *tablespoon Dijon mustard*
2 *tablespoons balsamic vinegar*
1/2 *cup olive oil*
  Salt and freshly ground black pepper
    to taste
1/2 *red onion, thinly sliced*
1/2 *cup finely chopped fresh parsley*

Place the potatoes in 2 separate saucepans. Cover with cold water and bring to a boil over medium-high heat. Reduce the heat and simmer about 20 minutes, or until the potatoes are tender when pierced with a fork. Drain the potatoes and set aside.

In a large mixing bowl combine the garlic, mustard, and vinegar. Gradually whisk in the oil. Season with salt and pepper. Gently fold the potatoes, onion, and parsley into the vinaigrette. Cover and chill overnight. Readjust the seasonings just before serving.

Morel Sauce for Fettuccine
Serves 4

Chef Tamara Murphy of Campagne in
Seattle, Washington, also serves this
creamy mushroom sauce over polenta.

- 3 tablespoons unsalted butter
- 1 tablespoon olive oil
- 1 garlic clove, minced
- 3 tablespoons chopped shallots
- 1 cup fresh morels
- 1 cup dry red wine
  Salt and freshly ground black pepper
- ¼ cup red wine vinegar
- ¼ cup brandy
- 3 cups chicken stock, preferably
  homemade
- 1 cup heavy cream
- 1 pound cooked fettuccine
  Freshly grated Parmesan cheese,

In a large skillet over medium heat, heat
the butter and olive oil. Stir in the garlic, 1
tablespoon of the shallots, and the mushrooms. Cook until the mushrooms are soft,
adding a little of the red wine as necessary
to prevent them from drying out. Season to
taste with salt and pepper. Remove the
mushrooms from the pan with a slotted
spoon and set aside.

Add the remaining shallots and the red
wine vinegar to the pan and simmer until
only 2 tablespoons of liquid remain, about 5
minutes. Add the remaining red wine and
the brandy; simmer until the mixture has
reduced to ¼ cup, about 10 minutes. Add
the chicken stock and simmer until the
sauce has reduced by one-third and coats
the back of a spoon, about 15 minutes. Add
the cream and simmer the sauce for 5 minutes on very low heat. Strain the sauce into
a clean saucepan. Stir in the mushrooms and
heat through. Serve over hot fettuccine
noodles and top with Parmesan cheese.

Recommended wine: *Merlot*

Venison with Blueberry-Vermouth Sauce
Serves 4

"Venison could be the meat of the 90s,"
says Gary Faessler. "It's delicious and, with
only 3 to 5 percent fat content and almost
no cholesterol, it's also very healthy. Unlike
beef, deer meat has no fat or marbling," he
says, "so choice cuts like the loin require
very little cooking. The meat should be
cooked rare to medium rare." Gary uses
organic fallow deer, a type of deer that has
been raised for food in Europe for more
than 5,000 years.

- 2 tablespoons olive oil
- 8 venison loin medallions, 1 inch thick
- 1 garlic clove, peeled and minced
- 2 rosemary sprigs, finely chopped
- 1 shallot, minced
- ⅔ cup dry red vermouth
- ¼ cup (½ stick) unsalted butter, chilled
- 1½ cups blueberries

Preheat the oven to 150° F.

In a large skillet, heat the oil over medium-high heat. Panfry the venison on both
sides, about 2 to 3 minutes per side. Transfer
the cooked venison to an ovenproof dish;
cover and keep warm in the oven.

Return the skillet to the heat. Add the
garlic, rosemary, shallot, and vermouth.
Deglaze the pan by stirring the liquid briskly
and incorporating any browned bits that
have gathered on the sides of the pan. Cook
the sauce over medium-high heat until it has
reduced about one-quarter, 8 to 10 minutes.

Add to the sauce any juices that may
have collected around the venison. Remove
from the heat and whisk in the butter a bit
at a time. Add the blueberries, return to the
heat, and warm through. Divide the sauce
evenly among 4 heated serving plates and
top with 2 venison medallions each.

Recommended wine: *Cabernet Sauvignon*

Blackberry Ketchup
Makes approximately 4 cups
(2 pints)

This old-fashioned blackberry ketchup from Chef George Poston of the Celilo Restaurant in Portland, Oregon, will keep up to 1 week in the refrigerator. It can also be canned and sealed for later use. If you choose to can the ketchup, be sure to follow reliable instructions for home canning. This makes a great condiment for venison or other wild game.

2½ pounds ripe blackberries (about 8 to 9 cups)
1½ cups firmly packed brown sugar
1¾ cups granulated sugar
2½ cups cider vinegar
2½ teaspoons ground cinnamon
2 teaspoons salt
1½ teaspoons ground ginger
1 teaspoon ground allspice
½ teaspoon ground cloves
¼ teaspoon freshly ground black pepper

Mix the berries, sugars, and vinegar in a heavy saucepan and heat until the mixture comes to a boil. Mash the berries with a potato masher or puree in a food processor until the berries are liquefied. Strain the berries through a sieve back into the saucepan, pressing the pulp with a wooden spoon. Add the cinnamon, salt, ginger, allspice, cloves, and pepper and reduce the mixture over low heat until it coats the back of a spoon, about 15 to 20 minutes. Ladle while still hot into ½-pint jars and refrigerate, or process in a hot water bath to preserve for a longer perior.

Red Chili, Pinot Noir, and Honey Marinade for Lamb, Pork, or Beef
Makes 1½ cups

Slather this thick, brick-red sauce on your favorite cut of meat and let it marinate for at least 2 hours or even overnight. Use the marinade to baste the meat as it grills. This is enough for 3 to 4 pounds of meat; any leftovers can be refrigerated for up to two weeks.

2 ounces (6 to 8) dried red chilis, mild to medium hot, such as ancho, mulato, or pasilla
2 teaspoons instant coffee granules
¼ cup honey
2 garlic cloves, minced
¼ cup olive oil
½ cup Pinot Noir or other dry red wine
1 teaspoon salt

Stem and rinse the chilis and place them in a mixing bowl. Add the instant coffee granules, pour boiling water over them, and let them soak for at least 1 hour, or until tender. Drain the chilis, reserving the soaking liquid, and puree them in a blender or food processor, adding reserved soaking liquid as necessary. Discard the remaining soaking liquid.

Transfer the chili puree to a mixing bowl. Stir in the honey, garlic, oil, wine, and salt. Cover tightly and store in the refrigerator.

Charcoal-Broiled Venison Steak

Serves 4

Venison, the meat of deer, elk, or moose, is delicious cooked over a barbecue with a simple gloss of olive oil and herbs. Serve it with Blackberry Ketchup (page 153).

> 3   *garlic cloves, peeled and minced*
> 1   *tablespoon chopped fresh rosemary*
> 2   *tablespoons olive oil*
> 4   *6-ounce venison steaks, 1 to 1½*
>   *inches thick*
>   *Salt and freshly ground black pepper*

Preheat the charcoal grill.

Mix the garlic, rosemary, and olive oil together and rub the steaks with this mixture, letting them sit ½ hour. Broil the steaks over hot coals 8 to 14 minutes, depending on the thickness of the steak and the rareness desired. Season to taste with salt and pepper.

Note: If desired, the steaks can be pan-broiled by searing them very quickly on both sides in a very hot skillet.

Recommended wines: *Cabernet Sauvignon, Merlot*

Spicy Blackberry Ketchup enhances grilled venison.

Heli-Skiing Picnic

Icy cold air blasts through the open windows as the helicopter sails up the narrow valley known as Porcupine Drain. Nearing the bowl of the drain, the helicopter turns, providing a sweeping view of the majestic North Cascade Mountains and the Methow River Valley below. The pilot shouts out the names of the nearby peaks—Cut Throat, Liberty Bell, Black Peak, Tower Mountain, and, at 8,896 feet in elevation, Silver Star Mountain.

We set down on a twenty-foot-wide shelf of snow with vertical drops of more than four thousand feet on either side. This high mountain ridge, with its breathtaking three hundred and sixty degree view and access to some of the region's most magnificent, untraveled ski slopes, is among Kathy and Randy Sackett's favorite spots for picnicking and heli-skiing, one of the Northwest's most spectacular sports.

The Sacketts own and operate North Cascades Heli-Skiing in north central Washington. Both native northwesterners, they met on Mount Rainier, where they worked as ski guides. After marrying, a search for a community in which they could work, raise a family and, most important, ski, led them to the Methow Valley.

Many of the Sacketts' heli-ski customers stay close by at the Sun Mountain Lodge, where upon request, the lodge's award winning chef, Jack Haynes, will pack a special heli-skiing picnic. With the fresh mountain air working as a natural palate cleanser, each bite of food tastes spectacular.

Randy Sackett carves an igloo-style table and benches out of snow and covers them with bright table cloths and cushions for picnicking.

Pork Medallions with Spiced Applesauce
Serves 4

"With a spoon, a pan, and your own good sense, you should be able to cook good food," says Susan Fletcher, who with her husband, Bill, runs the Turtleback Farm Inn on Orcas Island. Susan prefers fresh-from-the-farm flavors in her dishes. She accompanies pork with unsweetened applesauce made from Pippin, Northern Spy, and Jonagold apples grown in the family's orchard.

Marinade
- ¼ cup soy sauce
- 2 tablespoons Dijon mustard
- ½ cup dry sherry
- 2 garlic cloves, peeled and minced
- 2 tablespoons grated fresh gingerroot
- ½ teaspoon fresh thyme
- ½ teaspoon black pepper

- 8 boneless pork chops
- 2 tablespoons sherry
- 3 tablespoons fresh lemon juice
- 2 tablespoons soy sauce
- ½ cup mint jelly

Spiced Applesauce (recipe follows)

Combine the ingredients for the marinade in a nonreactive baking dish. Marinate the pork chops for ½ hour, turning once or twice. Drain the chops, reserving the marinade, and grill or broil the chops to the desired degree of doneness (this will depend on thickness), basting occasionally. Set the chops aside and keep warm.

Place the remaining marinade in a saucepan and bring to a boil over high heat. Boil until the sauce has reduced to 4 tablespoons, about 5 minutes. Stir in the sherry, lemon juice, soy sauce, and mint jelly; heat through and pour over the pork chops. Serve with Spiced Applesauce.

Recommended wines: *Pinot Noir, Zinfandel*

Spiced Applesauce
Serves 4

- 6 to 8 medium apples, unpeeled
  Sugar, to taste
- 2 tablespoons fresh lemon juice
- 3 tablespoons prepared horseradish

Wash, quarter, and core the apples. Place them in a saucepan and cover partially with water. Simmer until the apples are tender, about 20 minutes, then puree in a ricer or food processor, skin and all. Sweeten to taste with sugar and return to the saucepan. Cook for 3 more minutes. Stir in the lemon juice and horseradish and chill for at least ½ hour.

Roast Turkey Studded with Lemon and Onion
Serves 12

Don Thompson, who ran the Wave Crest Inn in Cannon Beach, Oregon, with his wife, Vie, described this turkey, pocketed with lemon and onion slices, as "looking like the devil." Don learned to cook this dish from a friend and after trying it once, he never cooked Thanksgiving turkey any other way.

- 1 10- to 16-pound turkey
- 3 lemons, seeded, halved lengthwise, and sliced ½ inch thick
- 3 onions, peeled and cut into 8 pieces
- 8 garlic cloves, peeled and mashed
  Salt and freshly ground black pepper
- ½ cup (1 stick) unsalted butter, melted
- ¼ cup sherry

Preheat the oven to 325° F.

Rinse and dry the turkey. With a paring knife, make deep slits, about ½ inch long and spaced about 3 inches apart, throughout the bird. Into these slits, insert slices of lemon and onion, making more slits as necessary, until the lemon and onion are used up. (The lemon and onion will stick partially out of the holes.) Fill the cavity of the turkey with the mashed garlic, rub the skin with salt and pepper, and place the bird, breast side down, in a roasting pan.

Combine the melted butter and sherry. Brush or spoon over the top of the turkey. Place the turkey, uncovered, in the oven and bake, basting often with the remaining butter, until the turkey is golden brown, about 1½ hours.

Turn the bird over. Baste with the pan juices and bake, basting often, until the breast side is golden brown and a meat thermometer inserted between the thigh and the body of the bird registers 190° F. (If not using a thermometer, allow approximately 15 minutes per pound.)

Let the turkey sit at room temperature for about 15 minutes before carving. Serve with the pan juices.

Recommended wine: *Pinot Noir*

Honey Curried Chicken
Serves 4

This flavorful curry, from Kathy and Randy Sackett of North Cascades Heli-Skiing, is especially good served over hot biscuits flavored with wild sage or saffron (page 148). It's also just as good—maybe even better—reheated, making it the perfect meal to end a long day of skiing. The chicken in this recipe needs to be precooked, which can be done up to 1 day in advance.

1 whole chicken (about 4 pounds)
6 cups cold water
1 teaspoon salt
¼ teaspoon freshly ground black pepper
¼ teaspoon crushed dried tarragon leaves
2 tablespoons vegetable oil
1 medium onion, chopped
3 tablespoons curry powder
3 tablespoons all-purpose flour
1 teaspoon powdered ginger
½ teaspoon salt
¼ cup soy sauce
¼ cup plus 2 tablespoons honey
¼ cup chopped toasted hazelnuts or
   almonds (page 82) (optional)

Place the whole chicken in a large kettle with the water, salt, black pepper, and tarragon. Bring the water to a boil over high heat, then reduce the heat and simmer, uncovered, until the chicken is tender, about 1 hour.

Remove the chicken from the liquid with a slotted spoon and let it cool until it can be handled. Strain the stock through a fine sieve. Reserve 3 cups in a small saucepan for the curry sauce and keep warm over a low flame. (The rest can be frozen for another use.)

While the chicken is cooling, heat the vegetable oil in a large skillet over medium heat. Add the chopped onion and sauté until the onion is golden brown, about 5 minutes. Reduce the heat to low and stir in the curry powder, flour, ginger, and salt. Continue cooking for 5 minutes over low heat, stirring constantly.

Gradually add the warm chicken broth to the curry mixture about 2 tablespoons at a time, stirring constantly. Next, stir in the soy sauce and honey, mixing well. Simmer the sauce over low heat for about ½ hour, or until thickened. In the meantime, skin and bone the chicken and tear the meat into bite-size pieces.

When the sauce has thickened, stir in the chicken meat and cook about 10 minutes more over low heat, or until the chicken is heated through.

Ladle the hot chicken curry over hot biscuits or rice and sprinkle with the nuts, if desired.

Recommended wines: *Riesling or Gewürztraminer*

Above: **Fresh-caught trout.**
Opposite: **Salmon-enhanced potatoes.**

Campfire Panfried Trout
Serves 4

There's no better breakfast than just-caught trout fried in butter, prepared over a camp-fire or a kitchen range. As the saying goes, "Cooked correctly, trout have only ONE bone"; by pushing the meat gently off each side of the fish, you can lift the tail, the bones, and the head off in one piece.

  8 *8-inch trout*
  2 *to 4 tablespoons unsalted butter*
      Salt
      Freshly ground black pepper

Starting just above the tail, slit each trout along its belly up to the gills. Make a small horizontal slit from the entry point at the tail through one side to butterfly the fish. Wipe the insides clean with paper towels.

Heat the butter in a cast-iron or heavy-bottomed skillet over medium-high heat until it sizzles. Reduce the heat to medium. Sprinkle the fish with salt and pepper and lay the butterflied trout flesh side down in the pan. Cook 2 or 3 at a time until golden, about 3 to 5 minutes. Flip the trout and cook until golden, about 3 more minutes. Serve hot.

Recommended beverage: *Beer*

Smoked Salmon Scalloped Potatoes
Serves 8

These creamy potatoes flavored with smoked salmon and Parmesan cheese are delicious for brunch served with scrambled eggs and freshly squeezed orange juice.

  10 *medium red potatoes, cooked, peeled,*
        and cut into ¼-inch slices
    6 *ounces smoked salmon, crumbled*
    6 *green onions, diced (reserve 2 table-*
       spoons for garnish)
    3 *garlic cloves, minced*
      Salt to taste
   ¾ *cup heavy cream*
   ½ *cup freshly grated Parmesan cheese*

Preheat the oven to 350° F. Grease an 8 x 13-inch baking dish or casserole.

Place a layer of sliced potatoes in the pan. Sprinkle with one-quarter of the smoked salmon, one-quarter of the onions, and one-quarter of the garlic; sprinkle with salt. Continue layering until all the potatoes, salmon, onions, and garlic are used up. Pour the cream over the casserole and top with the grated cheese. Bake for 40 minutes, or until golden. Sprinkle each serving with the reserved green onions.

Recommended wines: *Pinot Noir, Sauvignon Blanc*

Sourdough Starter
Makes approximately 2 cups

Having a sourdough starter is a must if you bake your own breads; it adds a wonderfully complex, old-world flavor. Until the late 1800s, when baker's yeast was first introduced by the Fleischmann brothers, breads were leavened solely with wild yeasts, naturally occurring airborne ferments that were cultivated in a sourdough mash made from potatoes, flour, and water. Each family kept its leaven alive by preserving a handful of dough each time they baked bread, and leavens were passed on from one generation to the next.

> 4 *large baking potatoes, peeled and diced*
> 2 *tablespoons sugar*
> 1 *cup unbleached all-purpose flour*

Place the diced potatoes in a saucepan. Cover with water, bring to a boil, and simmer until tender, about 12 minutes. Drain, reserving the cooking liquid. Mash the potatoes, adding the cooking liquid gradually. Stir in the sugar and flour, mixing well and scraping down the sides of the bowl. Cover with plastic wrap, then with a thick towel (this helps keep the starter warm). Set the starter in a warm place for at least 3 days, or until the mixture starts to ferment and becomes very bubbly.

The starter is now ready to be used. To store, place the starter in a large plastic container fitted with a lid (quart-size yogurt containers work well). With a paring knife make 8 or so slits in the lid to allow the sourdough to breathe. Store in the refrigerator (it will keep indefinitely if fed occasionally), but always allow the starter to warm to room temperature before using.

Replenish the starter each time it is used by reserving at least ¼ cup of starter. Stir in warm water and flour until a thick pancakelike batter is formed. Cover the starter loosely and let it sit at room temperature until it begins to bubble, then cover and store in the refrigerator.

Note: If you don't use the starter for more than a month, take it out of the refrigerator and warm it to room temperature. Stir in ½ cup flour and enough water to make a thick batter. Let it sit at room temperature until it begins to bubble, then cover and refrigerate.

Wild Mountain Huckleberry Tart with Sweet Hazelnut Pastry
Makes one 10-inch tart

There are five varieties of wild huckleberries native to the Northwest, all of which belong to the heath family (*Ericaceae*). These include wild mountain huckleberries (*Vaccinium ovatum*), as well as red huckleberries (*Vaccinium parvifolium*) and evergreen huckleberries (*Vaccinium ovatum*), among others. All of these berries are delicious and can be used interchangeably in recipes.

This sweet pastry makes a nice contrast to the tart huckleberry filling, which needs to cool before using. Blueberries or gooseberries make a fine substitute for the huckleberries in this recipe.

> **Filling**
> 4 *cups huckleberries*
> 2½ *cups sugar*
> ½ *cup unbleached all-purpose flour*
> ½ *cup water*
>
> **Pastry**
> 3 *cups unbleached all-purpose flour*
> ¾ *cup sugar*
> ¼ *teaspoon salt*
> ¾ *teaspoon cinnamon*
> ¾ *cup ground toasted hazelnuts (page 82)*
> 2 *teaspoons grated lemon rind*
> 1½ *cups (3 sticks) unsalted butter, chilled*
> 6 *large egg yolks*
> 4 *to 6 tablespoons ice water, as needed*

To make the filling, combine the huckle-berries, sugar, flour, and water in a large saucepan. Bring the mixture to a boil over medium heat, stirring often. Simmer until the berries become soft and slightly mushy, about 10 minutes. Turn into a bowl and cool to room temperature, or cover and refrigerate until needed.

For the pastry, combine the flour, sugar, salt, cinnamon, ground hazelnuts, and lemon rind in a mixing bowl. Cut in the butter until it is reduced to pea-size bits. Add the egg yolks and 4 tablespoons ice water, kneading lightly to form a stiff dough and adding more water as necessary to bind. Divide the pastry dough into 2 pieces. Wrap each piece in plastic and set aside for at least 15 minutes before using. (Allow the pastry to sit for a few minutes at room tem-perature if it has been chilled if for longer than 15 to 20 minutes.)

To assemble the tart, roll out half of the pastry 1/4 inch thick. Line a 10-inch tart pan with a removable bottom with the pastry. Spoon the cooled filling over the pastry and smooth the top. Roll out the remaining pastry and, using a fluted pastry wheel (or scissors), cut the pastry into 1/2-inch-wide strips.

Weave the strips in a crisscross pattern over the top of the tart. Trim the edges of the pastry to extend 1/2 inch beyond the rim of the pan. Fold the pastry under itself and crimp the edges. Chill the tart for 1/2 hour to firm up the filling and pastry.

Preheat the oven to 375° F. Bake the tart for about 35 to 45 minutes, or until the pas-try is golden brown. Let sit at least 1 hour before serving.

Huckleberry-Cream Cheese Pie
Makes one 9-inch pie

Use wild red or blue huckleberries, or sub-stitute cultivated blueberries in this cool, creamy pie from the Granger Berry Patch in Granger, Washington.

> 1 *cup granulated sugar*
> 1/4 *cup unbleached all-purpose flour*
> 1 *tablespoon fresh lemon juice*
> 3 *cups huckleberries*
> 3 *ounces cream cheese, softened*
> 1/2 *cup confectioners' sugar*
> 1/2 *teaspoon vanilla extract*
> 1/2 *cup heavy cream, whipped*
> 1 *baked 9-inch piecrust, cooled to room*
>   *temperature*

Combine the granulated sugar and flour in a medium saucepan. Stir in the lemon juice and berries. Bring to a simmer over medium heat and cook, stirring constantly, until thickened, about 10 minutes. Cool to room temperature.

In a mixing bowl, cream together the softened cream cheese and confectioners' sugar. Add the vanilla, then fold in the whipped cream. Spread the cream cheese mixture evenly over the baked piecrust and top with the cooled berries.

Chill at least 1 hour, or until set.

Horse Backpacking

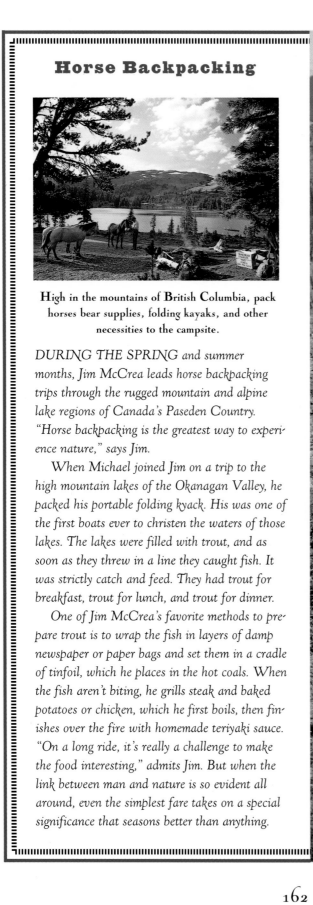

High in the mountains of **British Columbia**, pack horses bear supplies, folding kayaks, and other necessities to the campsite.

DURING THE SPRING and summer months, Jim McCrea leads horse backpacking trips through the rugged mountain and alpine lake regions of Canada's Paseden Country. "Horse backpacking is the greatest way to experience nature," says Jim.

When Michael joined Jim on a trip to the high mountain lakes of the Okanagan Valley, he packed his portable folding kyack. His was one of the first boats ever to christen the waters of those lakes. The lakes were filled with trout, and as soon as they threw in a line they caught fish. It was strictly catch and feed. They had trout for breakfast, trout for lunch, and trout for dinner.

One of Jim McCrea's favorite methods to prepare trout is to wrap the fish in layers of damp newspaper or paper bags and set them in a cradle of tinfoil, which he places in the hot coals. When the fish aren't biting, he grills steak and baked potatoes or chicken, which he first boils, then finishes over the fire with homemade teriyaki sauce. "On a long ride, it's really a challenge to make the food interesting," admits Jim. But when the link between man and nature is so evident all around, even the simplest fare takes on a special significance that seasons better than anything.

Blackberry Ice Cream
Makes 2 quarts

Nothing tastes more like summer than blackberry ice cream made from juicy, sun-ripened berries. Frozen berries can also be substituted. To freeze blackberries, spread them in a single layer on a baking tray and freeze until solid. Pack in plastic bags or freezer containers.

> 1 quart blackberries (thawed if frozen)
> ½ cup fresh lemon juice
> ¾ to 1½ cups sugar, to taste
> 1 tablespoon vanilla extract
> 4 large egg yolks
> 2½ cups heavy cream
> 2 cups half-and-half

Purée the blackberries with the lemon juice and sugar in a blender or food processor. Strain the puree through a fine sieve to remove the seeds. Whisk together the vanilla and egg yolks in the top of a double boiler. Gradually whisk in 1 cup cream. Cook gently over simmering water, stirring constantly. As soon as the mixture begins to thicken, remove from the heat and whisk in the rest of the cream and the half-and-half. Fold in the blackberry mixture. Freeze in an ice cream maker according to the manufacturer's directions.

Baked Winter Fruits
Serves 8

Spiced with candied ginger, cinnamon, and allspice and studded with walnuts, this flavorful fruit dish from the Turtleback Farm Inn on Orcas Island, Washington, is delicious served with yogurt for breakfast or as an accompaniment to pork or game.

> 1 pound dried apricots, halved
> 1 pound dried peaches, coarsely chopped
> 4 tablespoons (½ stick) unsalted butter
> 1¼ cups dry white wine
> 1 cup firmly packed dark brown sugar
> 1 teaspoon minced candied ginger
> 1 teaspoon vanilla extract
> Grated zest and juice of 1 lemon
> ¼ teaspoon ground cinnamon
> ¼ teaspoon ground allspice
> ¼ teaspoon ground ginger
> 1 cup chopped walnuts

Butter a 2-quart glass baking dish. Mix the dried fruits together. Place half of the fruit in the bottom of the prepared dish and dot with 2 tablespoons of the butter cut into small bits. Spread the remaining fruit on top and dot with the remaining 2 tablespoons of butter. Combine the wine, sugar, ginger, vanilla, lemon zest and juice, and spices. Blend thoroughly and pour over the fruit. Sprinkle with the walnuts and cover with foil. Refrigerate overnight.

One hour before baking, remove the fruit from the refrigerator. Preheat the oven to 375° F. Bake the fruit, covered, for about 45 minutes, or until it has plumped and the liquid has become caramelized. Uncover and cool. Serve at room temperature.

Northwestern Bed & Breakfasts

THERE ARE CHARMING bed and breakfasts located throughout the Pacific Northwest, where travelers can spend the night in home-style comfort and rise to a hearty home-cooked meal.

Many innkeepers in the Northwest are excellent cooks and pride themselves on serving foods fresh from their farms. Breakfasts cooked by Loragene Gaulin at the Country Cottage Bed and Breakfast in Roberts Creek, British Columbia, always begin with lots of French roast coffee and fresh fruit. Later come whole-grain waffles topped with freshly picked blackberries and mounds of hand-whipped cream, freshly baked lemon-pecan scones, and local Canadian bacon, all cooked on an antique wood stove.

At the Turtleback Farm Inn on Orcas Island, Susan Fletcher gathers farm-raised eggs each morning to use in her ham omelets and homemade crepes, which she smothers in a thick wild blueberry sauce. Susan also serves hand-pressed apple cider, multigrain waffles topped with real maple syrup, and homemade granola, which won a blue ribbon at the county fair. (See page 170 for a listing of bed and breakfasts in the Northwest.)

Pound Cake with Maple-Ginger Raspberries and Pears
Serves 4

Nina Wong of Vancouver, British Columbia, created this lovely fruit sauce flavored with maple syrup and candied ginger to serve over her mother's pound cake. Her recipe follows, but even over commercially prepared poundcake, this topping is heavenly.

> 2 tablespoons unsalted butter
> 4 pears, peeled, cored, and quartered
> 1/3 cup maple syrup
> 1/4 cup chopped candied ginger
> 1 cup fresh raspberries
> 4 3/4-inch slices of Catherine's Perfect Pound Cake (recipe follows) or purchased pound cake

Melt the butter in a large saucepan over medium heat. Sauté the pears just until they begin to soften, about 10 minutes. Add the maple syrup, ginger, and raspberries, reserving a few raspberries for garnish. Heat just until warmed through. Pour over the pound cake slices.

Catherine's Perfect Pound Cake
Serves 12

> 3 cups sifted all-purpose flour
> 1 teaspoon baking powder
> 2 cups (4 sticks) butter, softened
> 2 cups sugar
> 1 teaspoon vanilla extract
> 9 large eggs, separated

Preheat the oven to 325° F. Grease and flour a 10-inch tube pan.

Sift together the flour and baking powder, then resift 2 more times. In a mixing bowl, cream the butter, gradually adding 1 1/4 cups sugar, and continue beating until light and fluffy. Mix in the vanilla. Add the egg yolks one at a time, beating well after each addition. Mix in the flour mixture.

In another bowl, beat the egg whites until stiff. Gradually beat in the remaining 3/4 cup sugar. Fold the egg whites into the batter in 2 or 3 batches then spoon into the tube pan. Tap the pan firmly on the counter to release any air pockets. Bake about 1 hour and 10 minutes, or until a toothpick inserted in the center comes out clean. Cool in the pan 10 minutes before unmolding.

Above: **A** wedge of golden shortbread.
Opposite: **S**piced homemade cider.

Hazelnut Shortbread
S e r v e s   8   t o   1 o

Hazelnuts ripen in the fall, when the air is brisk and the sky is dazzling with leaves of crimson and gold.

Unshelled hazelnuts should be stored in a cool, dry place and will keep up to 1 month. Shelled, they will keep up to a month stored in the refrigerator in an airtight container, or they can be frozen for up to 6 months.

> 1 cup (2 sticks) unsalted butter, softened
> 2/3 cup confectioners' sugar
> 2 cups unbleached all-purpose flour
> Pinch of salt
> 1/2 teaspoon vanilla extract
> 1 teaspoon grated orange rind
> 3/4 cup ground toasted hazelnuts (page 82)
> 1/4 cup coarsely ground hazelnuts

Preheat the oven to 325° F. Lightly oil a 9-inch fluted tart pan with a removable bottom.

In a mixing bowl, cream the butter and sugar until light and fluffy. Sift together the flour and salt and add to the butter mixture. Stir in the vanilla, orange rind, and 3/4 cup ground toasted hazelnuts. Chill the dough for about 1 hour, or until firm.

Press the dough into the pan, leveling the top. Press the coarsely ground hazelnuts into the top. Score the shortbread with a knife, dividing it into 8 to 10 wedges. Bake the shortbread for 30 to 45 minutes, until the edges are golden and the middle is still soft. Cool and divide into wedges.

Spiced Cider with Apple Brandy
S e r v e s   6

When entertaining, Turtleback Farm Inn owner Susan Fletcher of Orcas Island, Washington, fills a Crockpot with this hot spiced cider and lets her guests serve them-selves, adding a jolt of brandy to taste. She prefers the apple brandy made by the Portland, Oregon–based Clear Creek Distillery. This brew will warm your bones on cold fall and winter evenings.

> 2 cinnamon sticks, broken in half
> 1 tablespoon allspice berries
> 3 whole cloves
> 1 quart apple cider
> 6 ounces (3/4 cup) apple brandy
>   (Calvados) or applejack
> 6 cinnamon sticks, for garnish

Tie the broken cinnamon sticks, allspice berries, and whole cloves together in a cheesecloth bag. Place in a 2-quart saucepan and add the cider. Heat slowly until very hot, but do not boil. Place 1 ounce of brandy and a cinnamon stick in each mug. Pour in the hot cider and stir with the cin-namon sticks to blend.

Directory of Sources and Locations

Oregon Department of Agriculture
Agricultural Development and
Marketing Division
121 S.W. Salmon, Suite 240
Portland, OR 97204-2987
(503)229-6734

Washington State Department of Agriculture
406 General Administration Bldg.,
AX-41
Olympia, WA 98504
(206)902-1800

Food Products

Anna Lena's Cranberry Products
Box 1399
Long Beach, WA 98631
1-800-272-6237
Dried cranberries and other cranberry
products

Antique Apple Orchard, Inc.
28095 Santiam Hwy
Sweet Home, OR 97386
(503)367-4840
More than 100 varieties of apples for
sale by mail order and retail sales

Bear Creek Artichokes
Tillamook, OR 97141
(503)842-4501
Contact: Bill and Cindy Miles
Artichokes, fresh produce, preserves

Boundary Bay Game Farm Ltd.
7225 Ladner Trunk
Delta, BC V4K 3N3
(604)946-4801
Fallow deer, bison, wild boar

Cascade Mushrooms
530 Northwest 112th Avenue
Portland, OR 97229
(503)294-1550
Wild mushrooms

Classic Country Rabbit
P.O. Box 1412
Hillsboro, OR 97123
1-800-821-7426
Fresh and frozen rabbit meat and
sausages

Clear Creek Distillery
1430 NW 23rd Avenue
Portland, OR 97210
(503)248-9740
Contact: Stephen McCarthy
Fruit brandies and grappas

The Creamery/Ferdinand's
Washington State University
Pullman, WA 99164-4418
(509)335-4014
Cougar Gold Cheese—extra sharp
Cheddar

Evonuk Oregon Hazelnuts
P.O. Box 7121
Eugene, OR 97401
(503)747-6887, 1-800-992-6887
Hazelnuts and hazelnut products,
including dry-roasted

Fresh & Wild
Box 2981
Vancouver, WA 98668
(206)737-3652
Free brochure. Wild mushrooms, sea
beans, salmon berries, fiddlehead
ferns, etc.

**The Granger
Berry Patch**
1731 Beam Road
Granger, WA 98932
(509)854-1413 or 800-346-1417
Contact: Ken and Sandy Fein
Honey-sweetened whole berry spreads
and syrups, sweet bing cherries, berry-
flavored honeys, fresh berries, etc.

The Herbfarm
32804 Issaquah-Fall City Road
Fall City, WA 98024
(206)784-2222 or 800-866-HERB
Contact: Ron Zimmerman and Carry
Van Dyke
Herbs, cooking and gardening classes,
seeds, cookbooks, and restaurant

Island Farmcrafters
Waldron Island, WA 98297
(206)739-2286
Organic garlic

Jake's Famous Products
4552 Southeast International Way,
Suite G
Milwaukie, OR 97222
(800)777-7179
Dungeness crab, salmon, crawfish

Mutual Fish Company, Inc.
2335 Rainier Avenue S.
Seattle, WA 98144
(206)322-4368
Salmon and crab

Northwest Chestnuts
265 Butts Road
Morton, WA 98345
(206)496-3395
Chestnuts in shell and frozen peeled
chestnuts

**Northwest Mushroom
Company, Inc.**
1-800-569-6101
Offers a variety of dried wild mushrooms, including morels, chanterelles,
porcini, and others

Northwest Select
14724 184th Street N.E.
Arlington, WA 98223
1-800-852-7132
Organic and wild greens, and herbs

Oakridge Organic Orchards
367 Oakridge Road
White Salmon, WA 98672
(509)493-3891
Contact: Dennis and Bonnie White
Organically grown apples and pears

**Oregon Hazelnut
Marketing Board**
Box 23126
Portland, OR 97223
1-800-503-NUTS
Resource for hazelnut recipes, sources,
and samples

Oysterville Sea Farms
P.O. Box #6
Oysterville, WA 98641
(206)665-6585
Contact: Dan Driscoll
Oysters and clams and smoked oysters

Quillisascut Cheese
(509)738-2011
Contact: Laura Lee Misterly
Handmade cheeses

Rising Sun Farm, Inc.
2300 Colestin Road
Ashland, OR 97520
(503)482-5392
Contact: Elizabeth Fujas
Pesto sauces, dried tomatoes, vinai-
grettes, fruit and herb vinegars, specialty mustards, etc.

Rogue Gold Dairy, Inc.
234 S.W. Fifth Street
Grants Pass, OR 97526
(503)476-7786
Eighteen varieties of cheeses, including
Blue, Cheddar, Jack, Smoked, and raw
milk Cheddar

Rogue River Valley Creamery
Box 3606
Central Point, OR 97502
(503)664-2233
Oregon Blue cheese

Rollingstone Chevre
27349 Shelton Road
Parma, Idaho 83660
(208)722-6460
Goat cheeses

Sally Jackson Cheeses
Star Rt. 1, Box 106
Oroville, WA 98844
(509)485-3722
Handmade cow, goat, and sheep's milk cheeses

Salumeria di Carlo
3739 SE Hawthorne Boulevard
Portland, OR 97214
(503)239-4860 or (503)221-3012
Handmade sausages, prosciutto, pepperoni

Tall Talk Dairy
11961 S. Emerson Road
Canby, OR 97013
(503)266-1644
Goat milk cheeses, yogurt, German and summer sausages

Taylor United, Inc.
SE 130 Lynch Road
Shelton, WA 98584
Fresh shellfish grown in Washington, including clams, Dungeness crab, spot prawns, and a variety of oysters, including native Olympias
For commercial orders contact:
Karen Johnson
(206)426-6178, ext. 25

For smaller quantities, contact: Xinn (pronounced Zin) Dwelley, ext. 27

Vancouver Island Seafood Specialties Ltd.
#404-999 Canada Place,
Vancouver, B.C.
Canada V6C 3E2
(604)984-3472
Variety of shellfish products

Walla Walla Gardener's Association
210 North 11th Street
Walla Walla, WA 99362
(800)553-5014
Walla Walla Sweet onions

Restaurants and Bed & Breakfasts

Campagne
Inn at the Market
86 Pine
Seattle, WA 98108
(206)725-2800

Captain Whidbey Inn and Restaurant
2072 W. Captain Whidbey Inn Road
Coupeville, WA 98239
(206)678-4097

Christina's
1 Main Street
Eastsound, Orcas Island, WA 98245
(206)376-4904

Country Cottage Bed & Breakfast
General Delivery
Roberts Creek, BC.
Canada VON 2W0
(604)885-7448

Dupuis Restaurant & Tavern
U.S. 101 Port Angeles, WA 98362
(206)457-8033

The Herbfarm Restaurant
See listing under food products

Higgins'
1239 S.W. Broadway
Portland, OR 97204
(503)227-3883

Kaspar's by the Bay
19 W. Harrison
Seattle, WA 98119
(206)298-0123

Pazzo Ristorante
627 S.W. Washington Street
Portland, OR 97205
(503)228-1515

Salishan Lodge
Highway 101
Gleneden Beach, OR 97338
(503)764-2371

The Shelburne Inn and
Shoalwater Restaurant
Pacific Hwy 103 & N. 45th Street
Seaview, WA 98644
(206)642-4142 (Shoalwater)
(206)642-2442 (Shelburne)

Sooke Harbour House and
Restaurant
1528 Whiffen Spit Road, R.R. 4
Sooke, B.C., Canada VOS 1NO
(604)642-3421

Table for Two Restaurant &
Briggs and Crampton Catering
1902 NW 24th Avenue
Portland, OR 97210
(503)223-8690

Turtleback Farm Inn
Rt. 1 Box 650
Eastsound, WA 98245
(206)376-4914

Westmoreland Bistro
7015 SE Milwaukie Avenue
Portland, OR 97202
(503)236-6457

Yarrow Bay Grill
1270 Carillon Point
Kirkland, WA 98003
(206)889-9052

Services

Carriage and Wagon Service
Contact: Liz Henderson and
John Keen
Keen's Cross J
1410 Kubli Road
Grants Pass, OR 97527
(503)846-7164

"Chefs About Town" TV
Cooking Show
Vancouver, B.C., Canada
COOKING SHOW
VIDEO TAPES
can be ordered through:
Rogers Cable T.V. Ltd.
Eaton Center Metrotown
1600-4710 Kingsway
Burnaby, B.C.
Canada V5M 4M5
(604) 430-5550

The Northwest Palate magazine
Box 10860
Portland, OR 97210
(503)224-6039

Heli-Skiing
North Cascades Heli-Skiing, Inc.
Box 367
Winthrop, WA 98862
(509)996-3272
Contact: Randy and Kathy Sackett

Horse Backpacking in British
Columbia's Wilderness Areas
Contact: Jim McCrea
Aldergrove, B.C. V4W 2H8
(604)856-5477

Index

Conversion Chart
Equivalent Imperial and Metric Measurements

American cooks use standard containers, the 8-ounce cup and a tablespopon that takes exactly 16 level fillings to fill that cup level. Measuring by cup makes it very difficult to give weight equivalents, as a cup of densely packed butter will weigh considerably more than a cup of flour. The easiest way therefore to deal with cup measurements in recipes is to take the amount by volume rather than by weight. Thus the equation reads:

1 cup = 240 ml = 8 fl. oz.   1/2 cup = 120 ml = 4 fl. oz.

It is possible to buy a set of American cup measures in major stores around the world.

In the States, butter is often measured in sticks. One stick is the equivalent of 8 tablespoons. One tablespoon of butter is therefore the equivalent to 1/2 ounce/15 grams.

Liquid Measures

FLUID OZ.	U.S.	IMPERIAL	ML
	1 TSP	1 TSP	5
1/4	2 TSPS	1 DESSERTSPOON	7
1/2	1 TBS	1 TBS	15
1	2 TBS	2 TBS	28
2	1/4 CUP	4 TBS	56
4	1/2 CUP OR 1/4 PINT		110
5		1/4 PINT OR 1 GILL	140
6	3/4 CUP		170
8	1 CUP OR 1/2 PINT		225
9			250, 1/4 LITER
10	1 1/4 CUPS	1/2 PINT	280
12	1 1/2 CUPS OR 3/4 PINT		340
15		3/4 PINT	420
16	2 CUPS OR 1 PINT		450
18	2 1/4 CUPS		500, 1/2 LITER
20	2 1/2 CUPS	1 PINT	560
24	3 CUPS OR 1 1/2 PINTS		675
25		1 1/4 PINTS	700
27	3 1/2 CUPS		750
30	3 3/4 CUPS	1 1/2 PINTS	840
32	4 CUPS OR 2 PINTS OR 1 QUART		900
35		1 3/4 PINTS	980
36	4 1/2 CUPS		1000, 1 LITER
40	5 CUPS OR 2 1/2 PINTS	2 PINTS OR 1 QUART	1120
48	6 CUPS OR 3 PINTS		1350
50		2 1/2 PINTS	1400
60	7 1/2 CUPS	3 PINTS	1680
64	8 CUPS OR 4 PINTS OR 2 QUARTS		1800
72	9 CUPS		2000, 2 LITERS
80	10 CUPS OR 5 PINTS	4 PINTS	2250
96	12 CUPS OR 3 QUARTS		z2700
100	5 PINTS		2800

Solid Measures

U.S. and Imperial		Metric	
OUNCES	POUNDS	GRAMS	KILOS
1		28	
2		56	
3 1/2		100	
4	1/4	112	
5		140	
6		168	
8	1/2	225	
9		250	1/4
12	3/4	340	
16	1	450	
18		500	1/2
20	1 1/4	560	
24	1 1/2	675	
27		750	3/4
28	1 3/4	780	
32	2	900	
36	2 1/4	1000	1
40	2 1/2	1100	
48	3	1350	
54		1500	1 1/2
64	4	1800	
72	4 1/2	2000	2
80	5	2250	2 1/4
90		2500	2 1/2
100	6	2800	2 3/4

Suggested Equivalents and Substitutes for Ingredients

all-purpose flour—plain flour
arugula—rocket
beet—beetroot
confectioners' sugar—icing sugar
cornstarch—cornflour
eggplant—aubergine
granulated sugar—caster sugar
kielbasa—Polish sausage
lima beans—broad beans
pearl onions—pickling onions
scallion—spring onion
shortening—white fat
snow pea—mangetout
sour cherry—morello cherry
squab—poussin

squash—courgettes or marrow
unbleached flour—strong, white flour
vanilla bean—vanilla pod
zest—rind
zucchini—courgettes
light cream—single cream
heavy cream—double cream
half and half—12% fat milk
buttermilk—ordinary milk
sour milk—add 1 tablespoon vinegar or lemon juice to 1 cup minus 1 tablespoon lukewarm milk. Let stand for 5 minutes.
cheesecloth—muslin

Oven Temperature Equivalents

FAHRENHEIT	CELSIUS	GAS MARK	DESCRIPTION
225	110	1/4	Cool
250	130	1/2	
275	140	1	Very Slow
300	150	2	
325	170	3	Slow
350	180	4	Moderate
375	190	5	
400	200	6	Moderately Hot
425	220	7	Fairly Hot
450	230	8	Hot
475	240	9	Very Hot
500	250	10	Extremely Hot

Any broiling recipes can be used with the grill of the oven, but beware of high-temperature grills.